ART EXPERIENCE

M. HIRIYANNA

INDIRA GANDHI NATIONAL CENTRE FOR THE ARTS
NEW DELHI

MANOHAR
2026

First published 1954

New edition 1997
Reprinted 2026

ISBN 978-81-7304-180-8

Published by
Indira Gandhi National Centre for the Arts,
Janpath, New Delhi 110001,
an association with Ajay Kumar Jain *for*
Manohar Publishers & Distributors
4753/23 Ansari Road, Daryaganj
New Delhi 110 002

Printed and bound in India

Contents

Publishers' Note to the First Edition

This is the third volume of Prof. Hiriyanna's essays to be published. All the papers collected here—including a few review articles—are devoted to a consideration of the problems of Aesthetics. Of these, two studies—*Indian Aesthetics—2* and *Art and Morality*—are being published here for the first time; the others have appeared from time to time, in various journals and publications.

Corrected copies of the essays left by the author have been made use of in editing the volume and the marginal notes found in the papers have been, as far as possible, incorporated either as part of the text or as footnotes. In the few instances where it was found necessary by the editors to add a word or two, these have been enclosed within square brackets. Articles with identical titles have been numbered 1 and 2, for purposes of essay reference.

We are deeply grateful to the late Prof. Hiriyanna's daughter who placed at our disposal all the papers needed in the editing of the volume. We are under a deep debt of gratitude to Prof. T. N. Sreekantaiya of the Karnatak University, Dharwar, a former pupil of Prof. Hiriyanna, who gladly took upon himself the editorial responsibility of this collection including the reading of proofs. Our thanks are due to Sri N. Sivarama Sastry of the University of Mysore, who has been extremely helpful editorially; to Sri R. K. Narayan who has been helpful in many ways; and to the authorities of the Wesley Press and Publishing House who have spared no pains to make the volume handsome.

Acknowledgements

I am grateful to Messrs. *George Allen and Unwin Ltd.*, for their courtesy in allowing me to include in this collection my late father Prof. Hiriyanna's article *Art Experience* appearing in *Radhakrishnan: Comparative Studies in Philosophy presented in honour of his sixtieth birthday.* My thanks are also due to the Secretaries of the *All-India Oriental Conference*, the Registrars of the *Universities of Madras* and *Mysore* and the Registrar of the *Annamalai University*, the Editors of the *Indian Review*, the *Aryan Path* and *The Hindu* and the Authorities of the *Adyar Library, Madras*, who readily gave permission to include in the present volume the several essays and reviews first published by them.

M. R.

FIRST PUBLICATION

Indian Aesthetics—1: *Proceedings of the First All-India Oriental Conference*, 1919.

What to Expect of Poetry? *Mysore University Magazine*, 1923.

Art Contemplation: *Indian Review*, 1946.

Art Experience—1: *Aryan Path*, 1941.

Art Experience—2: *Radhakrishnan: Comparative Studies in Philosophy presented in honour of his sixtieth birthday. Allen and Unwin*, 1951.

The Number of Rasas: Foreword to *The Number of Rasa* by Dr. V. Raghavan. *The Adyar Library, Madras*, 1940.

The Problem of the Rasavadalaṁkāra: *Proceedings of the Fifteenth All-Indian Oriental Conference*, 1949.

Some Aspects of Literary Criticism in Sanskrit. [= Rasa and Dhvani]: *Journal of the Madras University*, 1929.

The Philosophy of Aesthetic Pleasure: *Journal of the Annamalai University*, 1941.

Studies of some Concepts of the Alaṁkāra Literature: *Journal of the Madras University*, 1942.

Sanskrit Poetics: *The Hindu*, 8 October 1944.

Process and Purpose in Art: *Aryan Path*, 1944.

Experience: First and Final: *Aryan Path*, 1948.

Foreword

For decades *Art Experience* has been a lamp which has provided illumination to many a serious student of Indian aesthetics. It first appeared in 1919. At that time there was a general acceptance of the view that while there were many philosophic schools in India, aesthetics was not the concern of any of the systems. Alongside was the heated debate on the nature of Indian art. Ruskin, Birdwood, William Archer and Sri Aurobindo had crossed swords. In many essays now included in *Foundations of Indian Culture*, Sri Aurobindo denounced these mistaken notions. A.K. Coomaraswamy joined the debate first in defence and later to expound the metaphysics which governed the art.

Although the text of the *Nāṭyaśāstra* had been located, neither authentic editions nor the commentary of *Abhinava Bhāratī* became the subject of serious discourse in the disciplines of either philosophy or aesthetics.

A contemporary of the late Dr. S. Radhakrishnan, M. Hiriyanna was steeped in Indian philosophy and known for his precision, scrupulousness and economy of expression. He was the first amongst the pioneers to establish meaningfully the relationship of philosophy, aesthetics and life. As if in a flash of incisive insight, Hiriyanna pointed at the core concept of the Upaniṣadic view which was as relevant to philosophy as to art. The central point of this view, he said 'is that whatever is one . . . is manifested most clearly in the inner self of man than in the outer world'. This, he added, brought about a total revolution, for it led directly to the enunciation of the absolute kinship of Nature and Man. This observation had far-reaching implications for the critical discourse in both philosophy and art. Of equal significance was his penetrating statement.

The world of sense equally with the world of thought is but an appearance of the ultimate truth, an imperfect expression of it, but yet adequate if rightly approached to point at the underlying unity. Through a few precise sentences M. Hiriyanna turned the pattern of the discourse on Indian art and aesthetics from histories, chronologies and mythologies, monotheism and pantheism to its fundamentals of a world view, and the diverse paths of the quest for truth, *viz.*, through speculative thought or, alternately, refinement of senses and sense perceptions. Also it was Hiriyanna who sharply pointed at the relevance of the concept of the *jīvanmukti* here and now and not a life hereafter or world beyond to the whole field of Indian art. He highlighted the Indian view that achievement of a life of harmony was not through extinguishment of interests but by an expansion of them through training and refinement of feeling and the cultivation of emotion. The simple lucidity of these deep insights into the Indian tradition was as fresh and unconventional at that time as authentic and pure.

A generation of scholars have carried these observations as a talisman for investigating the contours of Indian aesthetics, be it a V. Raghavan, K.C. Pandey or Krishnamurthy or others. Hiriyanna had, as if in one gentle stroke, cleared the path for others to walk steadily without fear of taking on defensive positions.

Consequently, over these decades many vistas have opened up for interpreting Indian aesthetics on its terms at the deepest level. No longer is it necessary to understand Indian aesthetics by referring to Plato, Aristotle and others. Nor is it any longer necessary to prove that there is a long and a most sophisticated philosophic discourse on aesthetics.

These essays, particularly 'Indian Aesthetics I' and 'Indian Aesthetics II', are thus landmarks in scholarship on Indian aesthetics. Although Hiriyanna does not discuss the interpretation of the theory of Rasa from other philosophic schools, he elucidates the theory from the point of Sāṅkhya in a masterly fashion.

Equally important are the other essays on Rasa and Dhvani, Sanskrit poetics, and forewords (e.g. all foreword to Dr. V. Raghavan's books on the number of Rasas). Each essay illuminates a facet of Indian aesthetics or an aspect of poetics. They are like glow-worms in a dark night, flashes of insight in an inimitable style of conciseness and pithy economy of words. There is no weight of heavy or cumbersome scholarship, footnoting and referencing. They thus stand a class apart from all those others whose work is characterised by erudition and information. For the reader, be he a Sanskritist or not, they make engaging reading and are full of contemporary relevance.

It was thus with the greatest pleasure and enthusiasm that I responded to Sri H.Y. Sharada Prasad's suggestion that the collection be reprinted. For me personally this is an occasion to pay a tribute to one to whom I am deeply indebted. For it was his writing, along with that of A.K. Coomaraswamy's, which turned the course of my own pursuits from Western aesthetics to Indian aesthetics. Some sentences of the essay on 'Indian Aesthetics Part I' have been like mantras which reveal multiple meanings each time they are read and reflected upon.

I am also deeply grateful to Sri Sharada Prasad for translating with his usual sensitivity the essay by the great scholar Sri D.V. Gundappa, on M. Hiriyanna. This is a very moving piece of writing which brings us in touch with the man and the scholar M. Hiriyanna. The essay has greatly enriched the volume. It is clear from this essay as well as from other essays in this volume and Hiriyanna's book *Indian Conception of Values* that for M. Hiriyanna 'Experience was first and last'. He wrote from experience and not merely erudition. This filters through unmistakably in all his writing.

I would like to record the IGNCA's thanks to Kavyalaya Publishers, Mysore (holders of the copyright) for permission to reprint the essays and to Manohar Publishers & Distributors, New Delhi, our copublishers.

14 August 1996 KAPILA VATSYAYAN

1

Indian Aesthetics—1

IT HAS BECOME somewhat of a commonplace in these days to speak of the ancient Hindus as having achieved distinction in philosophy. But the word 'philosophy' is so loosely used and the phases of philosophic investigation are so many and so varied in character that such an opinion, standing by itself, cannot be taken to indicate anything beyond a certain aptitude of the Hindu mind for abstract speculation. A signal illustration of the indefiniteness of this opinion is furnished by Max Müller, the very scholar that was largely responsible for giving currency to the view that the ancient Hindus were highly gifted philosophically; for while he at one time described them as 'a nation of philosophers', yet, at another time, gave out as his considered opinion that 'the idea of the beautiful in Nature did not exist in the Hindu mind.'[1] The fact is that a vague and general statement like the above is of little practical value unless it is supported by evidence of progress made in the various departments of philosophic study, such as logic, psychology and metaphysics. Here is a vast field for the student of Indian antiquities to labour in and the harvest, if well garnered, will be of advantage not only for the history of Indian thought but also, it may be hoped, for Universal Philosophy. The object of the present paper is to indicate, however slightly it may be, the nature of the advance

[1] See *The Philosophy of the Beautiful*, by William Knight, Part I, p. 17.

made by the Indians in one bye-path of philosophy, *viz.*, aesthetics or the inquiry into the character of beauty in Nature as well as in art.

The most noticeable feature of Indian philosophy is the stress which it lays upon the influence which knowledge ought to have on life. None of the systems that developed in the course of centuries in India stopped short at the discovery of truth; but each followed it up by an inquiry as to how the discovered truth could be best applied to the practical problems of life. The ultimate goal of philosophic quest was not knowledge (*tattvajñāna*) so much as the achievement of true freedom (*mokṣa*). Indian philosophy was thus more than a way of thought; it was a way of life; and whoever entered upon its study was expected to aim at more than an intellectual assimilation of its truths and try to bring his everyday life into conformity with them. Consistently with this pragmatic aim, ethics occupies a very important place in Indian philosophy. Like ethics, aesthetics is dependent upon philosophy and like ethics, it aims chiefly at influencing life. When such is the kinship between ethics and aesthetics, is it probable that a people who devoted so much attention to one of them, altogether neglected the other? Is it conceivable that they who showed special power in the grasp of the good did not even stumble upon the kindred conception of the beautiful? We are not however left to such vague surmises; for, not infrequently we find in Sanskrit philosophical works[2] parallels drawn from art which imply that the close relation of the beautiful to the good and the true was not all unknown to ancient India. We have even more direct evidence in the numerous works in Sanskrit on poetics which, though their set purpose is only to elucidate the principles exemplified in poetry and the drama, yet furnish adequate data for constructing a theory of fine art in general. A consideration of the teachings of these works shows us that Indian aesthetics had its own history; and the process of its evolution, as may well be expected, followed closely that of general philosophy.

It is well known that the earliest philosophy of India consisted

[2] Compare, e.g. *Sāṁkhya-kārikā*, st. 65; *Sāṁkhya-tattva-kaumudī* on st. 42, 59; and *Pañcadaśī* of Vidyāraṇya, ch. X.

in the explanation of the universe by means of a number of supernatural powers called *devas*, 'the shining ones', or 'gods'. This pluralistic explanation however soon appeared inadequate to the growing philosophic consciousness of the Indian; and a quest began thereafter whose aim was to discover the unity underlying the diversity of the world. The history of this quest is very long and can be traced from the *Mantras*, through the *Brāhmaṇas*, down to the period of the *Upaniṣads*. Various principles were in turn regarded as representing this ultimate reality—some concrete, others abstract—and although each solution was in turn given up as unsatisfactory, the search itself was not abandoned until an abiding conclusion was reached in what is known as 'the *ātman* doctrine' of the *Upaniṣads*. The central point of this doctrine is that whatever is, is one; and that its essence is manifested more clearly in the inner self of man than in the outer world. This doctrine brought about a total revolution in the point of view from which speculation had proceeded till then; for the ultimate reality was no longer regarded as something external but as fundamentally identical with man's own self. The enunciation of the absolute kinship of Nature with Man marks the most important advance in the whole history of Indian thought. I am not, however, for the moment, concerned with this philosophic solution in general, reached in the Upaniṣadic period. I am interested only in emphasising one aspect of it, *viz*., that what we commonly regard as real is not in itself the ultimate reality but only a semblance of it. The world of sense, equally with the world of thought, is but an appearance of the ultimate truth—an imperfect expression of it but yet adequate, if rightly approached, to point to the underlying unity. Neither our senses nor our mind can grasp this unity, but so much of it as they can grasp is sufficient to find out its true meaning and realise it within ourselves.

There is a second aspect of Indian philosophy to which it is necessary to draw attention before speaking of Indian art. The earliest philosophy of India had a supernatural basis. Although the objects of early Aryan worship were in reality only powers of Nature, there were supposed to be working behind them supernatural beings. So long as this belief continued, the ambition of the Indian in this life was to secure the favour of those beings with a view to attain companionship with them hereafter. This eschatological view changed with the change of belief in the gods, but yet for long afterwards there lingered the view that the highest good that man could attain was attainable only after death. With an ideal like this, man naturally looked upon the present life as merely a passage to another and a better one. He lived mainly for the coming world, disregarding, if not altogether discarding,. the realties of this life. Asceticism was the natural outcome of it. In course of time this ideal of practical life also underwent a change, not less important than the change on the speculative side to which I have already referred and it came to be believed that the highest ideal that man could attain was attainable on this side of death, here and now. The full development of this view belongs to the period that followed the composition of the classical *Upaniṣads* but its source can be traced earlier in those Upaniṣadic passages which refer to *jīvanmukti.*[3] *Jīvanmukti*, to speak from the purely philosophic standpoint, marks the highest conception of freedom. It is one of the points where Indian philosophy emerges clearly from Indian religion; for, the goal of existence according to this conception is not the attainment of a hypothetical bliss *hereafter* but the finding of true freedom on this bank and shoal of time. It is difficult to exaggerate the importance of this change. It transformed the whole outlook of the Indian upon life and remoulded his ethical ideal. The ideal, not doubt, was yet as far as ever from the average man; but what once was more or less a matter of pure speculation had been brought within the possibility of positive experience. The aim of life was no longer conceived as something to be sought for beyond this world, but to be realised *here*, and if one so willed, *now*. The new ideal was the achievement of a life of harmony, not through the extinguishment of interests but by an expansion of them—not through repressing natural impulses but by purifying and refining them. It was a mode of living characterised by passionless purity and an equal love for all, such for

[3] The word *jīvanmukta* is not known to the *Upaniṣads*; but the conception is there all the same. Cf., e.g. *Kaṭha Up.* II. ii. 1., II. iii. 14.

instance as is described in glowing terms more than once in the *Bhagavadgītā.*[4] For the realisation of this ideal, the training of the feelings was a necessary preliminary and in consequence, the first aim of life came to be looked upon not so much the cultivation of the intellect or the development of the will, as the culture of the emotions.

In these two characteristic features of early Indian philosophy, it seems to me, we have the main influences which moulded the theory of art as it is disclosed to us in Sanskrit works on poetics. We do not know when this class of works began to appear. Tradition is at one[5] in counting Bhāmaha among the earliest writers on poetics; but in him we see the subject has already assumed a definite shape. His name, along with those of some others like Udbhaṭa Rudraṭa, Daṇḍin and Vāmana is associated with a distinctive canon of poetry. There are indeed differences in matters of detail among these writers. For instance, there is no clear distinction recognised between *guṇas* and *alaṁkāras* by some,[6] while others give the one or the other of these the first place in judging the worth of a poem.[7] It is not necessary to enter into these details here; for all these writers, in spite of minor differences, exhibit cognate ways of thinking. We may therefore regard them as, on the whole, representing the first stage in the growth of poetic criticism. In the writers of this *prācīna* school we find the subject of poetry dealt with under three heads—*doṣas, guṇas,* and *alaṁkāras*. The last, *alaṁkāras*, may be left out of consideration here; for, in the first place, they are not recognised by all to be essential, and in the second, they almost exclusively relate to imaginative literature and have no proper place in any general theory of art. Some of the conditions laid down under the remaining two heads are intended only to secure logical or grammatical requirements such as coherence of thought and correctness of language. Even the others as we shall presently see, rarely allude

[4] e.g. v. 23–5.

[5] Comp., e.g. the first śloka of the *Pratāparudrīya; Alaṁkāra-sarvasva* (Nir. S. Pr.), p. 3.

[6] e.g. by Udbhaṭa (see *Alaṁkāra-sarvasva* by Ruyyaka, p. 7).

[7] See Vāmana: *Kāvyālaṁkāra-sūtra*, III. i. 1, 2 and 3.

to the central essence of poetry. Where they do involve a reference to this essence, its importance is misjudged and only a subordinate place is assigned to it.[8] The attention of this school is practically confined to the outward expression of poetry, *viz.*, *śabda* (word) and *artha* (sense). Certain forms of these are regarded as *doṣas* and certain others as *guṇas*; and it is held that what confers excellence on poetry is the absence of the one and the presence of the other.

There is another school known as the later or *navīna* school of critics, the theory advanced by whom is far different. As in the case of the earlier school, this also seems to have had more than one branch. We shall here consider the most important of them as represented by the *Dhvanyāloka*. Apparently it is the oldest work of the kind extant; but this very work contains evidence of the fact that the point of view which it adopts in judging poetry had been more or less well known for a long time before.[9] This work starts by distinguishing between two kinds of meaning—the explicit and the implicit—and attempts to estimate the worth of a poem by reference to the latter rather than to the former.[10] The explicit meaning, no less than the words in which it is clothed, constitutes, according to this view, the mere vesture of poetry.[11] They together are its outward embodiment—the necessary conditions under which a poetic mood manifests itself. These external and accidental features alone appealed to the earlier school. But the critic of the new school concentrated his attention on the implicit meaning which forms the real essence of poetry. From this new standpoint things like *doṣas* or *guṇas*, in settling the nature of which there was once so much controversy, are easily explained. It is as though we are now in possession of the right key to the understanding of all poetry. Whatever in sound or sense subserves the poetic end in view is a *guṇa*; whatever does not, is a *doṣa*.[12] *Doṣas* and *guṇas* are

[8] Vide *Alaṁkāra-sarvasva* by Ruyyaka, pp. 3–7; *Dhvanyāloka*, pp. 9–10.

[9] Vide śloka i. 1; iii. 34, 52; also the final śloka of the *Āloka*.

[10] Vide *Dhvanyāloka*, i. 3–5.

[11] Ibid., i. 7–12.

[12] Cf. *Dhvanyāloka*, ii. 6.

relative in character. There is no absolute standard of valuation for them. They are to be judged only in reference to the inner meaning which constitutes the truly poetical. The artist never really feels concerned about them; for, a thought or feeling experienced with poetic intensity is sure to find expression. The expression is also likely to be more or less imperfect, but the question is not whether it is perfect, but whether it is adequate to convey the thought or emotion to others. If it is adequate it is good poetry, otherwise it is not.

The implicit meaning is threefold and the poet may aim at communicating a fact (*vastu*) or transferring an imaginative (*alaṁkāra*) or an emotional mood (*rasa*). The first is obviously the least poetic and whatever artistic character it may possess is entirely due to treatment and not to subject. We may, therefore consider here only the remaining two, which have their bases respectively in imagination and feeling. True art is no doubt a compound of feeling and imagination but in any particular case the one or the other may predominate and the twofold classification should be regarded as having reference to the predominant factor. In this view art represents the almost spontaneous expression of a responsive mind when it comes under the spell of an imaginative or an emotional mood. It was this expression—the outward element of poetry and not its inner springs which the older school of critics analysed.[13] The later school, as we have already seen, occupied itself with what this expression signifies. The expression was important to them only as a means of suggesting or pointing to the implicit significance. Here we find a theory of art which exactly corresponds to the doctrine of *ātman*. Just as the passing things of experience are not in themselves real but only imperfect manifestations of reality, so word and explicit meaning are but the exterior of poetry and until we penetrate beneath that exterior, we do not reach the poetic ultimate.

So far we have considered the essence of poetry as consisting in the imaginative thought or the emotional mood which a poet succeeds in communicating to us. But gradually more stress

[13] See *Dhvanyāloka*, iii. 52.

came to be laid upon the latter than upon the former. Under the influence of the altered ethical ideal to which allusion has been made above art came to be more and more utilised as a means of emotional culture. There was peculiar fitness in its being so used, for it cannot only teach, but also please and while it can successfully persuade, it can keep its persuasive character concealed from view. It was thus that poetry came to be viewed as possessing a double aim—the direct one of giving aesthetic delight (*sadyaḥparanirvṛti*) and the indirect one of contributing toward the refinement of character.[14] This particular use to which art was put made *rasa* more important than either *vastu* or *alaṁkāra*.[15] It is this change in the nature of Sanskrit poetry that is meant when it is stated that *rasa* is the *ātman* of poetry—a statement which by the way shows clearly the dependence of this canon on the *ātman* doctrine of the *Upaniṣads*. When the predominance of *rasa* came to be insisted upon as indispensable to artistic excellence, many of the systems of philosophy applied their own fundamental principles to its interpretation so that in course of time there came to be more than one theory of *rasa*. I shall devote the rest of the paper to an elucidation of these theories according to two of the chief systems, *viz*., Vedānta and Sāṁkhya alluding incidentally to the corresponding conceptions of beauty in Nature.

And first as regards the Vedānta. Among the various approximate terms used in the *Upaniṣads* to denote *Brahman*, one is *ānanda*. *Ānanda* means bliss; and *Brahman* according to the monistic and idealistic teaching of the *Upaniṣads*, represents the inner harmony of the universe. *Brahman* is termed *ānanda* because of the restful bliss that results from realising that harmony. *Brahman* is so termed for instance in the *Tait. Up*. iii. The appropriateness of the term *ānanda* consists just in this suggestion that the harmony of the universe must be realised in one's own experience and not merely intellectually apprehended; for there can be no such thing as mediated *ānanda*. This word

[14] Cf., e.g. *Kāvya-prakāśa*, i. 2.
[15] Cf., e.g. *Dhvanyāloka*, p. 27 (com.).

contains the clue to the whole aesthetic theory of the Vedānta. Common experience takes for granted that variety is the ultimate truth. According to the Vedānta, the final truth lies in the unification of this variety through a proper synthesis. But this unification is what takes place in perfect knowledge. Commonly we are occupied with appearances which give only a fragmentary view of reality. They alone concern us in our everyday life. But he who attains perfect knowledge—the *jīvanmukta*—transcends this fragmentary view. He may continue to perceive variety; but it ceases to have any ultimate significance for him. He merges in the unity which he realises all separate existence including his own and enjoys *ānanda*—the peace that passeth understanding. This higher viewpoint is not possible for us while we are yet on the empirical plane. We are absorbed in the narrow distinction between the self and the not-self. But sometimes, though rarely, there is a break in this routine and then in the sudden transition from one empirical state to another, we transcend our narrow selves. Our connection with the work-a-day world seems to snap. We do not indeed realise then, like the knower, the unity of all that is, but we yet resemble him in one respect, in that we lose sight of ourselves and feel delight, however short-lived it may be.

But among the myriad impressions that reach us from the outer world what is it that gives rise to such an attitude? This question admits of a variety of answers. It is now symmetry, now novelty, and now something else; and it is this variety that accounts for the almost bewildering number of theories of the beautiful that one finds in any history of aesthetics. According to the Vedānta, these do not constitute true beauty at all but are only its outward and visible symbols. Though diverse in themselves they point to the same underlying harmony which constitutes real beauty. But, this perfect beauty which is identical with the ultimate reality is revealed only to the knower. We perceive only its outward symbols and we may describe them as beautiful in a secondary sense, since we experience *ānanda* at their sight. Those who identify beauty with these external factors and seek it as an attribute forget that while these are perceivable by the senses, beauty is disclosed only to the 'inward eye'. True beauty is neither expressible in words nor knowable objectively; it can only be realised.

Beauty in Nature then, as we commonly understand, is anything that brings about a break in the routine life and serves as a point of departure towards the realisation of delight. This is the only condition which it should satisfy. But what is the significance of this break? Generally we lead a life of continuous tension, bent as we are upon securing aims more or less personal in character. In Śaṁkara's words life is characterised by *avidyā-kāma-karma*, i.e. desire and strife, arising out of the ignorance of the ultimate truth. When we are not actively engaged we may feel this tension relaxed; but that feeling of relaxation is deceptive for even then self-interest persists as may be within the experience of us all. Delight means the transcending of even this inner strain. The absence of desire then is the determining condition of pleasure; and its presence, that of pain. The absence of desire may be due to any cause whatever—to a particular desire having been gratified or to there being, for the time, nothing to desire. The chief thing is that the selfish attitude of the mind—the 'ego-centric predicament'—must be transcended at least temporarily, and a point of detachment has to be reached before we can enjoy happiness. Joy or bliss is the intrinsic nature of the self according to the Vedānta, that being the significance of describing the ultimate reality as *ānanda*. The break in the routine life restores this character to the self. If its intrinsic nature is not always manifest, it is because desire veils it. When this veil is stripped off, no matter how, the real nature of *ātman* asserts itself and we feel the happiness which is all our own. In the case of a *jñānin* the true source of this delight is known; but even when such enlightenment is lacking we may experience similar delight. We may enjoy while yet we do not know. To use Śaṁkara's words again, the ever-recurring series of *kāma* and *karman* or interest and activity constitutes life. The elimination of *kāma* and *karman* while their cause *avidyā* continues in a latent form, marks the aesthetic attitude; the dismissal of *avidyā* even in this latent form marks the saintly attitude. Thus the artistic attitude is one of disinterested contemplation but not of true enlightenment while the attitude of the saint is one of true enlightenment and disinterestedness but not necessarily of passivity. The two attitudes thus resemble each other in one important respect, *viz.*, unselfishness.

And now as regards the Vedāntic theory of *rasa*. The immediate aim of art, as already indicated, being pure delight, the theory of *rasa* in the Vedānta will be known if we ascertain the conditions that determine a pleasurable attitude of the mind. The overcoming of desire is the indispensable condition of pleasure. The artist has therefore to induce an attitude of detachment and he can easily do it by means of the ideal creations of his art. Being products of fancy they cannot awaken desire and when attention is once concentrated upon them, the ordinary state of tension caused by selfish desires is relaxed and joy ensues as a matter of course. The various devices of art such as rhythm, symmetry, etc., are intended to help this concentration and successfully maintain it. They also serve another important purpose, *viz.*, securing unity to the subject portrayed. We have seen that the knower who enjoys perfect beatitude realises unity in Nature's diversity. Similarly in artistic perception also, which is followed by pure delight, there is a realisation of unity in variety. But while in the one case what is realised is the truth of Nature, it is in the other the truth of art. The latter, no doubt, is a lower truth; but there is yet a close resemblance between the two attitudes; and we may well compare the person appreciating art to a *jīvanmukta*. He does indeed get a foretaste of *mokṣa* then; but it is not *mokṣa* in fact because it is transient, not being based upon perfect knowledge.

To turn to the Sāṁkhya: the essential features of this system are its dualism and its realism. It starts with two absolutes which are altogether disparate—*Prakṛti* and *Puruṣa*. The former splits up on the one hand into the entire psychic apparatus, with *buddhi* as its main factor; and, on the other, into the physical world constituted out of the five elements. The *Puruṣa* or self is awareness, pure and simple. It stands at one extreme while at the other is the objective world. The whole of the mental apparatus is designed to bring about a mediation between them. How *buddhi*, itself a product of *Prakṛti*, can serve as a connecting link between them—how a physical stimulus is converted into a physical experience—is a question which we need not stop to discuss. Our concern is not primarily with Sāṁkhya psychology or metaphysics but only with its conception of art. It is enough for our purpose if we remember that by such meditation *buddhi* enables the *Puruṣa* to realise either of the two ideals of life—*bhoga* and *apavarga*—that is, to experience pleasure and pain or to attain spiritual aloofness through right knowledge.

It is also necessary to make a brief reference here to the theory of the three *guṇas*. The conception of *guṇas* is as difficult to understand as it is essential to the system. Of the large number of effects[16] that can be traced to these *guṇas, sukha, duḥkha* and *moha*, which are respectively the result of *sattva, rajas* and *tamas*, are the most important; and it is possible that the Sāṁkhya system is less concerned with the intrinsic nature of things than with their meaning for us. It seems to aim primarily at estimating the value[17] of things as means of pleasure and pain and may therefore be described as a philosophy of valuation. Two applications of the doctrine of *guṇas*, we have to notice in particular here: (i) Everything whether it belongs to the outer physical world or to the inner psychic apparatus is made up of these three factors. But some are predominantly *sāttvic*, others predominantly *rājasic* or *tāmasic*. The *buddhi* is intrinsically *sāttvic* in this sense.[18] We must, however, remember that each individual *buddhi* has in it, from the beginning, *vāsanās* or acquired impulses which may modify its intrinsic *sāttvic* character and transform it into a predominantly *rājasic* or *tāmasic* entity. (ii) The feeling of pain or pleasure which we experience arises from the

[16] Vide quotation from *Pañcaśikhā* in *Sāṁkhya-pravacana-bhāṣya*, i. 127.

[17] Since no value has any meaning apart from consciousness, we probably have here an explanation for the persistent effort of certain orientalists to describe the Sāṁkhya philosophy as idealistic.

[18] What is meant is that *buddhi* when purged of all its egoistic impulses as in the case of a *jīvanmukta*, is *sāttvic*. Compare *Sāṁkhya-tattva-kaumudī* on st. 65; *Maṇiprabhā* on *Yogasūtras*, I. 49; and *Sāṁkhya-pravacana-bhāṣya*, ii. 15.

interaction of the two spheres of *prākṛtic* development—the *buddhi* on the one hand and the objective world on the other, the *Puruṣa* standing by, only as an onlooker. Though the *buddhi* owing to its intrinsic *sāttvic* character should give rise only to pleasure, the play of its acquired impulses coupled with the character of the particular physical object acting upon it may reverse this result. The same thing may therefore affect different persons differently. What causes pleasure to one may cause pain to another, and what one regards as beautiful, another may regard as ugly; everything that is perceived comes to be viewed through the distracting medium of individual purpose, and we ordinarily live in a secondary world, ignoring the intrinsic nature of things and setting a conventional value upon them according to our individual bias.

Now according to the Sāṁkhya, the basic cause of this predicament is to be traced to a mistaken identification of the *buddhi* with the *Puruṣa*. The mistake cannot be avoided until the *Puruṣa* dissociates himself from *buddhi* altogether, but, according to the Sāṁkhya, the question of neither pleasure nor pain arises then. So far as the ordinary empirical state is concerned, individual purpose or selfish desire is ineradicable and life becomes a condition of pain mixed with uncertain pleasure. What is pleasant to one may be unpleasant to another; or even to the same person at a different time. He, on the other hand, who acquires true knowledge and realises the intrinsic disparateness of *Prakṛti* and *Puruṣa* transcends the sphere of pain as well as of pleasure. Such a man is a *jīvanmukta*. He sees things not as related to him but as related among themselves, that is, as they are absolutely. Everything impresses him in the same way and nothing excites his love or hatred so that he is able to maintain complete composure of mind, and be, as Vijñābhikṣu says, serene like a mountain-tarn.[19]

But such absolute detachment is beyond the reach of ordinary man; for he cannot transcend his *buddhi*. He cannot therefore grow impersonal even for a while. But we should not therefore consider that the average man cannot escape from pain at all: for

[19] *Sāṁkhya-sāra*, vii. 16.

although he cannot transcend his *buddhi*, he can, by resorting to art, find a temporary release from the natural world, the second of the two factors contributing to the misery of ordinary existence. Pleasure untainted by sorrow does not exist in the real world and has therefore to be sought outside it. The world of art is no doubt like Nature, but being idealised it does not evoke our egoistic impulses. There we have a distinct class of things altogether, which are not made up of the three *guṇas*. They cannot give rise to either pleasure or pain. The mind is thus enabled to assume a well-poised attitude of which the automatic result is a feeling of pleasure. The artist's function is thus to restore equanimity to the mind by leading us away from the common world and offering us another in exchange.

I have stated that in not a few systems of philosophy, there was a deliberate application of fundamental principles to the interpretation of *rasa*. The distinctive doctrines of more than one system are found mentioned in Sanskrit works on poetics.[20] As an illustration of them, I shall take up the theory of *rasa* associated with the name of Bhaṭṭa Nāyaka and show how it is identical with the Sāṁkhya theory as briefly sketched above.[21] Bhaṭṭa Nāyaka was a reputed *ālaṁkārika* and wrote a work known as *Hṛdaya-darpaṇa* which, I believe, has not been discovered yet. But references to it are plentiful in *alaṁkāra* works, especially in Abhinavagupta's commentary on the *Dhvanyāloka*. Bhaṭṭa Nāyaka does not seem to have been much older than Abhinavagupta himself. The following is a *resume* of the theory as given in the *Kāvya-prakāśa*:

na tāṭasthyena nāmagatatvena rasaḥ pratīyate notpadyate nābhivyajyate api tu kāvye nāṭye cābhidhāto dvitīyena vibhāvādisādhāraṇīkaraṇātmanā bhāvakat-vavyāpāreṇa bhāvyamānaḥ sthāyī sattvodrekaprakāśānandamayasaṁvidviśrāntisatattvena bhogena bhujyate // (iv.)

If we leave out the references to the other views from which

[20] The commentary on *Ālaṁkāra-sarvasva* refers to as many as a dozen theories. (Vide p. 9.)

[21] The *Kāvya-pradīpa* identifies this theory as the one corresponding to the Sāṁkhya.

the present theory differs, there are three points worthy of note here:

(i) The first refers to the nature of the objects contemplated in art. They have no reference to anybody in particular. In life everything is consciously or unconsciously related to the individual perceiver (*ātman*) or to some one else (*taṭastha*); but the creations of art are wholly impersonal. It is not given to the ordinary man to transcend personal relations; art by its impresonalised forms affords the best means for a temporary escape from the ills of life arising from such relations.

(ii) The next point refers to three stages in the appreciation of poetry which gradually lead up to aesthetic experience. The first of them is the apprehension of the meaning of the words of a poem; the second the finding through them of generalised conceptions unrelated to any one in particular and lastly the actual experience of delight. This statement brings out clearly the characteristic of the Sāṁkhya theory that aesthetic delight is the result of contemplating the imaginative and therefore impersonal creations of the poet. In the passage quoted above these three states are represented as *vyāpāras* or processes ascribable to a work of art. The first of them is *abhidhā* by means of which the words constituting a poem convey their ordinary meaning. The second is *bhāvanā*.[22] It is the process of impersonalising by virtue of which the accessories of the emotion portrayed such as the *vibhāvas* become generalised (*sādhāraṇīkṛta*) thereby gaining a power of equal appeal to all. The words and their literal meanings are not therefore to be regarded as important in themselves but only as pointing to these generalised ideas. The third or *bhogīkarana* is that by virtue of which we are enabled to derive pure pleasure—*bhoga*—from these idealised creations of the artist. The purpose of evolution in the Sāṁkhya is *bhoga* and

[22] The word *bhāvanā* reminds one of *Mīmāṁsā* and it is possible that Bhaṭṭa Nāyaka was indebted to that system of philosophy for this conception. He was, we know from Abhinavagupta, a *Mīmāṁsaka*. In one of his many unkind remarks against Bhaṭṭa Nāyaka, Abhinavagupta suggests this. Cf. *Dhvanyāloka*, p. 63.

apavarga and the use of this word *bhoga* in this passage constitutes a link connecting the present theory with the Sāṁkhya. What is implied by the use of this word here is that the artistic attitude in spite of its being the source of unalloyed pleasure is more akin to the empirical than to the saintly attitude. Of these three *vyāpāras* the first is recognised by all. But it appears strange that the remaining two should be ascribed to a work of art. If however we remember that this theory is based on the Sāṁkhya we see that the statement is not altogether inappropriate. The *Puruṣa* according to the Sāṁkhya conception is absolutely passive so that all activity must be of *Prakṛti. Prakṛti* not only creates everything but also brings about *Puruṣa*'s experience of pleasure and pain through them, by means of its own agency. Thus *Prakṛti* discharges two functions: (*a*) that of evolving the things through which pleasure or pain may be derived, and (*b*) that of enabling *Puruṣa* to experience such pleasure and pain. These two steps may be seen in art also, if we distinguish the apprehension of idealised forms from the aesthetic enjoyment derivable from them. There is no doubt a touch of personification in the manner of its statement by Bhaṭṭa Nāyaka: but that is probably to be attributed to a desire to maintain the parallelism with Sāṁkhya metaphysics.

(iii) The third point refers to the nature of the aesthetic attitude itself. This attitude is one of *saṁvit*, i.e. contemplation dissociated from all practical interest as is shown by *viśrānti*—'composure'. Thus the artistic attitude differs from the natural as well as the spiritual attitude; for while the former is not always pleasurable and the latter neither pleasurable nor painful art produces a condition of pure pleasure. We have here the expression *sattvodreka* which is important inasmuch as it contains another indication of the theory being based upon Sāṁkhya philosophy.

To sum up the essential differences between the Vedānta and Sāṁkhya aesthetics. According to pessimistic Sāṁkhya, Nature is not wholly beautiful but has in it phases of beauty as well as of ugliness. It does not indeed say the objects in Nature do not give delight at all. What it means is that there is nothing in Nature which at all times is pleasurable to all. For pure unalloyed pleasure we must therefore look elsewhere than in the real world. According to optimistic Vedānta on the other hand everything is beautiful and there is nothing in the universe to mar its inward harmony. This is indeed the first corollary of the *ātman* doctrine and the saint is the greatest artist, for everything delights him. Although we may not possess the saint's knowledge that everything is *ātman*, we can occasionally derive aesthetic enjoyment from Nature. But ordinarily we are too dull to perceive the beauty of the universe. The artist who is endowed with an eye for the beautiful derives pleasure from Nature where we cannot and through the expression which he spontaneously gives to his feeling, he opens our eyes to what we miss. In a sense this art is Nature herself presented in such a manner that it appeals to us. The aim of art according to both the systems is to induce a mood of detachment. But according to idealistic Vedānta the artistic attitude is characterised by a forgetting, though temporary, of our individuality; while according to realistic Sāṁkhya, it is due to an escape from the natural world. According to the former, art serves as a pathway to Reality; but according to the latter, it is so to speak a 'deflection' from Reality. The one reveals the best in Nature, while the other fashions something better than Nature.

I must in conclusion say a word in regard to my selecting a subject which may appear to some as rather out of the way. Research has till now been largely confined to linguistic, historical and similar aspects of oriental learning; but there are still other aspects of it which cannot be regarded as either less instructive or less interesting. It appears necessary in the future not only to carry research further in the departments already worked, but also to widen considerably the sphere of research itself. What I have attempted in this paper does not profess to be more than a first and a very imperfect sketch of the subject I have selected; but I trust it is sufficient to indicate what vast fields of ancient Indian learning lie unexplored.

2

What to Expect of Poetry?

THERE ARE NUMEROUS works in Sanskrit on poetics, and with their help chiefly it is proposed here to find an answer to the question: What are we to expect from poetry? The consideration of this question presupposes a knowledge on our part of what poetry is; but we need not attempt anything so rash as to define that term. There are, as may be expected, several definitions of poetry to be found in these ancient books. They are neither better nor worse than those one meets with in modern works on the subject and we do not therefore cite any of these definitions, but shall content ourselves merely with pointing out the meaning of the Sanskrit word for poetry, *viz.*, *kāvya*. This word, it may be noted in passing, is equally applicable to verse as well as to prose; and it is explained as *kavi-karma*, which amounts to saying that poetry is what the poet writes. So far as the nature of poetry is concerned, this explanation is not very illuminating. It is useful, however, in this respect that it shifts the question from poetry to the poet; and it seems much less difficult to say what the Indians thought of the poet than of poetry. The common view of the poet is to regard him as a creator or maker; but there is also another, according to which his foremost aim is not to invent anything new but to represent life as it is—'to hold the mirror up to nature' as it is said. Of these, it is only the former view we come across in Sanskrit poetics. The poet as conceived here is not to rest content with merely copying Nature or life. His skill does not consist in selecting the salient features of an existing situation and portraying them exactly as they are, but rather in creating new situations. These situations will of course be modelled upon Nature; for the ideal, as Bain long ago observed, needs, like paper-currency, to rest always on a sufficient basis of the real. But at the same time, the poet's work involves the invention of many new elements; and it is for this reason that in Sanskrit literature the poet is often found compared to the Creator and the Creator to the poet.

So much about the Indian conception of the poet. But it takes two to make a poem, as some one has said; and we must now add a few words about the other party to it, *viz.*, the reader of poetry. A fit reader of poetry is known in Sanskrit as *sa-hṛdaya* which word will tell us all that we need know about him. The second element of this compound—*hṛdaya* means 'heart' and the first stands for *samāna*, i.e. 'same' or 'similar', so that the whole word signifies 'one of similar heart'. That is, the poet and the reader of poetry are of the same temperament. Both possess what is known as the 'poetic heart'; and its possession is the most important qualification of the reader of poetry. This identity of temperament between the two is assumed throughout Sanskrit poetics and the process of appreciating poetry is looked upon as essentially the same as producing it. Hence we frequently find Sanskrit writers describe the poet and the reader of poetry by the same set of terms. There is perhaps nothing very novel in the kinship here noticed; the point is that it receives particular emphasis in Indian works. The identity of temperament between the two means no doubt a certain restriction of the circle of competent readers of poetry; but there seems to be a good deal of truth in the restriction, for there is no warrant for assuming that the aesthetic sense is universal.

In this affinity between the poet and the reader of poetry we find a clue to the answer to our question. Every lover of poetry in this view is virtually a poet. Both possess, as already stated, the poetic heart, though it pulses much lower in the one than in the other. The poet, while he is under the finer influences of life, feels so intensely and vividly that his feeling spontaneously finds utterance. We, on the other hand, under similar circumstances are almost dumb. The lack of expression in us does not, however, necessarily mean that there is nothing to express. We also respond to such influences in our own way, but the resulting experience is faint and vague—so much so that we can hardly call it ours until it is properly articulated for us by the poet. Poetic feeling without poetic expression—that is why we do not by ourselves reach the truly poetic level, that is where we stand in need of the poet's assistance. The tiny stream also is to reach the ocean, but it is too feeble to do so without mingling with a mighty river. So we may say that it is for a fuller self-revelation that we seek the aid of poetry. This is, however, only a part and, comparatively speaking, a minor part of the answer to our question. It is true that the thoughts and feelings enshrined in poetry are sometimes the same as ours, finding clear and beautiful expression there; yet surely it would be absurd to say that we always went to the poet to have our own experiences unfolded to us. There is another and a far more important answer to our question and to discover it we have to recur to the conception of the poet as a creator.

What is the significance of this conception? and what in particular is the point in comparing the poet to the Maker of the universe? We need not discuss here whether the world as created by God is perfect or imperfect. What matters for us now is that the poet's world should be perfect. If the world of Nature also is perfect, it is certain we commonly miss the perfection or at best only catch a passing glimpse of it. This tragic aspect of our life has been splendidly expressed by a modern English poet in the following lines:

'Fate from an unimaginable throne
Scatters a million roses on the world,
They fall like shooting stars across the sky
Glittering. Under a dark clump of trees
Man, a gaunt creature, squats upon the ground
Ape-like and grins to see those brilliant flowers
Raining thro' the dark foliage; he tries
Sometimes to clutch at them, but in his hands
They melt like snow. Then in despair he turns
Back to his wigwam, stirs the embers, pats
His blear-eyed dog and smokes a pipe and soon
Wrapped in a blanket, drowses off to sleep.'

It is the peculiar glory of the poet that he never loses sight of these 'brilliant flowers'. He has always his eyes on the joy and beauty of the universe; and in his poems constructs for us new situations through which we are enabled to see and understand them. The function of the poet in this respect may be illustrated by that of a scientist who, discovering for himself a truth of Nature, hidden from the common view, devises a special apparatus to enable others to see that truth as clearly as he himself has done. It is not the truth of Nature that is invented here but only the medium through which it is revealed to us. Similarly in creating a new world, the aim of the poet is to reveal to us the inner significance of the world of Nature. This conception of the poet as a revealer is implied in the Sanskrit word for him, *viz.*, *kavi* itself, which occurs as early as the *Ṛg-Veda*. Philologists trace the word to a parent root from which the English verb 'show' also is descended. Thus *kavi* literally means 'one that shows' and he who shows must necessarily have himself *seen*. We may in this sense understand our word *kavi* as the equivalent of 'seer'. He portrays Nature, not as it is commonly known, but as it ought to be; and it is the vision of the true word we get through his work that is, according to this view, the source of our satisfaction in reading poetry. If instead of this we suppose the world of Nature to be imperfect and to contain evil with good, ugliness with beauty, the poet has to fashion something better than it, so that in his work at least man may find joy untainted by sorrow. This is the implication of passages in certain works on Sanskrit poetics where the poet is *contrasted* with the Creator. The *Kāvya-prakāśa*, one of the best known works on the subject, begins with such a contrast and describes the work of the poet in such well-chosen words that he is easily made out to be the more skilful to the two. According to both view-points, the poet ought to be a creator—only while in the one, the forms he creates disclose to us the truth of Nature commonly obscured, but yet there; in the other, they present for our contemplation something that is superior to Nature and is not there.

If such be the impulse behind poetry, what is it that we may seek from it? The answer must be twofold in accordance with the twofold explanation we have just given. If it is from an optimistic standpoint that we look as it, it is to draw ourselves closer to the intrinsic truth and beauty of the universe that we seek the aid of poetry; if from the pessimistic, it is to draw ourselves away from the sufferings and perplexities of actual life. In either case we are transported as it were from our usual surroundings and, moving in a world which the poet's fancy has called into being, we forget ourselves. Then we resemble the poet most: the only difference is that while he attains that condition spontaneously, ours is induced by him. It is this transcending of self-consciousness—this migrating from our narrow self, to put it otherwise, that constitutes the secret of aesthetic delight. The highest function of the poet who easily rises to this mood is to communicate the same to us. As the alchemist's herb is said to change even a common thing at once into gold, so the poet metamorphoses us instantly. He cannot indeed pass on to us his inspiration, but the poetic experience itself—its result, he can; and thereby he becomes our supreme benefactor. It is this wholly unique experience that is termed *rasa* in Sanskrit; and it is for attaining it that we almost instinctively go to poetry. That is the chief answer which we find in Sanskrit poetics to our question: What have we to expect of poetry?

Poetry then is to be regarded first and foremost as a means of securing a spell of detachment from common life and not for any lessons or 'criticism of life' it may contain. There is no doubt that it has many such lessons for us and that their value is great. But they are only the further good resulting from poetic experience and not the good which that experience itself is. Poetry represents an attitude, it also yields certain results; and the attitude is not less important than the results which follow from it. The time we devote to the reading of poetry, we must never forget, is itself a part of our life. It is necessary to lay stress on this point, for there is commonly some confusion between the reading of poetry and its uses. Indian writers have always clearly discerned the difference between the two and have recognised the reading of poetry as more an end in itself than as a means to something else. That is the underlying truth of the conception of *rasa*. This *rasānubhava* or aesthetic experience is to be preferred not only to whatever good may result from it, but also, in one sense, to the very writing of poetry; for as a Sanskrit *śloka* has it—'If you are not conversant with the best of poets—the kings among them—*how* can you purpose to write poetry? and, if you are, *why* should you?'

3

Art Contemplation

ALTHOUGH ART, IN one sense, may be concerned with the very essence of reality, it is clear that the persons and things with which it immediately deals, like the characters it describes or the scenes of external nature in which it presents them, are by no means real. But they are not therefore to be reckoned as illusions in the ordinary sense of the word, for they never mislead us. We merely *entertain* them, as it is said, neither believing nor disbelieving in them. The example commonly given by Indian writers in this connection is that of a painted horse (*citra-turaga*). We speak and think of it as a horse; but, all the time, we know that it is not one. This characteristic of art implies that it can have no bearing upon our activity, for all activity is directed towards real objects. In illustrating this fact, *viz.*, that the content of art lies outside actual life, a well-known Shakespearian scholar has stated that 'we dismiss the agony of Lear in a moment, if the kitten goes and burns its nose'.

This dissociation of art from our practical interests often gives rise to a misapprehension that the contemplation of the aesthetic object is quite passive. People take for granted that beauty is given ready-made in a work of art, and that we have merely to yield ourselves entirely to its influence to derive delight from it. Any effort that may be required on our part, they think, is restricted to keep out from our mind distracting factors that may wake us to a sense of the actual world from which we have withdrawn ourselves for the time being. This is not the view of uninstructed laymen alone; it sometimes receives support from even writers of standing in the field of art criticism. Thus Addison, referring to 'the pleasures of the imagination' by which he means the pleasures that may arise from the contemplation of nature or of art, speaks of the ease with which they can be secured. They require, he says, 'very little attention of thought or application of mind in the beholder'.[1]

What is overlooked in this naïve view, as we may call it, is the essentially creative character of art. So far as the artist is concerned, it is not difficult to see the need for constructive power. Even in realistic art, where he is supposed to be reproducing what is given in Nature and not aiming at the creation of beauty, he has to exercise a good deal of activity in the form of selecting, from among the features presented, those that are fit for portrayal and properly unifying them. For Nature, even at its best, contains irrelevant features, if not also ugly or disagreeable ones. To paint a landscape is more than to photograph it. The painter does not reproduce it as it is, but as his imagination represents it to him. In other words, the artist never copies the given mechanically, but idealises it; and in this idealisation lies the secret of his art. In the case of the spectator, doubtless, not such effort is necessary; for there are the aids, which the genius of the artist has provided, to guide him in his contemplation.[2] But the process should still involve activity, inasmuch as a proper appreciation of a work embodying the results of idealisation is impossible without an imaginative reconstruction of its content. It is only when thus ideally reconstructed that the beauty of the work becomes actual for the spectator; and it is only when it is thus 'verified by his own heart', as the Sanskrit expression goes, that he, rising above the interests of common life, forgets himself and is said to realise the aesthetic end. To put the same in the Indian way, the beautiful as a value needs to be striven for and

[1] Grant Allen also holds the same view. See William Knight's *The Philosophy of the Beautiful*, vol. 1, p. 250.

[2] This is at best the significance of the view that art contemplation is passive, when, e.g. Bhaṭṭa Nāyaka says so. [See Abhinavagupta's commentary on the *DA*., p. 29.]

achieved (*sādhya*), no matter whether one approaches it as an artist or as a spectator.[3]

This view of art contemplation entirely transforms the idea of the aesthetic end. In the naïve view alluded to above, the end is delight, to which contemplation is but a means; and the contemplation is justified by the end to which it leads. But here no such dualism of end and means is recognised. There is only a single self-justifying process of contemplation, which represents a *progressive* appreciation of the aesthetic object. The purpose is thus present throughout the process or is immanent in it;[4] and, if we look upon its culminating stage as the result, it is because that stage is marked by the repose of achievement.[5] The value of art accordingly consists not in providing mere delight for us, but in the totality of experience for which aesthetic contemplation stands. The feeling of pleasure is, no doubt, there, but only as an aspect of that experience. This is the significance of the term *rasa*, used in Sanskrit for aesthetic value—a term which literally means 'savour' or 'savouring' and implies that art valuation is an active process of which delight is only a characteristic feature. It is therefore wrong to think that art exists for our delectation. If it did, some at all events would not attach much importance to it. It aims rather at inducing in us a unique attitude of mind which signifies not only pleasure but also complete disinterestedness and a sympathetic insight into the whole situation depicted by the artist. The uniqueness of this attitude will become clear when we mention that, in the view of Indian thinkers, it is comparable to the ideal state of the *jīvanmukta* or one that has realised the goal of life.

We have stated that art has no aim beyond itself; but it may appear that this is not consistent with fact, since it is found

[3] This contemplation, we should add, is positive and therefore over and above the negative one whose aim, as stated earlier, is to enable us to continue to be in the peculiar atmosphere of art in which we have placed ourselves.

[4] Hence the familiar expression 'art for art's sake'. It means that art has no purpose beyond itself, and not that it has none at all.

[5] Cf. *Viśrāntidhāmatva of rasa: Dhvanyāloka-locana-kaumudī* (KSRI Edn), p. 102.

actually utilised in various spheres of life. For example, it has been used to further the interests of religion in all countries and in all ages. But this is only an apparent inconsistency. When we say that art is its own end, we think of the aesthetic process as integral and self-sufficing, so that its purpose is included in it. Art may have other purposes also, like the one to which allusion has just been made. But the point to be particularly noted is that, however excellent such purposes may in themselves be, they are external to art and possess no aesthetic value.[6] To give an illustration from the parallel realm of conduct, the ethical value of a good deed consists in the *doing* of it and in the right direction of the will involved in it. Any consequences that may follow from the deed are extraneous to it; and they, as students of the *Gītā* will well realise, have no direct bearing upon that value. One and the same work of art may have both these aims. But it takes away nothing from its worth if, while fulfilling its intrinsic purpose, it does not serve as a means to an external end. If, however, the reverse holds good in any case, e.g. a poem that is purely didactic, we may still value it for its usefulness but not as art.

[6] The category of means and end is relevant here, for art is conceived as instrumental in attaining these purposes.

4

Art Experience—1

THE EAGERNESS WITH which people visit places like theatres and music-halls shows the intrinsic attractiveness of art. We shall not attempt here the difficult task of accounting for this attractiveness, but shall only draw attention to some of the features that are distinctive of the enjoyment of art with a view to indicating its place, in the scheme of human experience. In the first place, the contemplation of a work of art leads to an attitude of mind which is quite impersonal. Whatever strain or conscious effort may be required for getting into that attitude, when once it is attained man forgets himself altogether; and he will be aware then of nothing beyond the object or the situation portrayed by the artist. In the second place, and probably as a consequence of such self-forgetfulness, the contemplation of art yields a kind of spontaneous joy. In both these respects, the aesthetic attitude stands higher than that of common or everyday life, which is generally characterised by personal interests of one kind or another and therefore also involves a variable degree of mental tension. It is for this reason that Indian philosophers, especially the Vedāntins among them, compare the experience of art with that of the ideal state which they describe as *mokṣa*. But the two experiences are only of the same order and not identical, for the former has certain limitations which are not found in the latter.

To begin with, art experience is transient. It does not endure long but passes away sooner or later, for it depends for its continuance upon the presence of the external stimulus which has evoked it. The ideal state, on the other hand, if it should answer to that description at all, must, when attained, necessarily become a permanent feature of life. Its attainment consequently means the rising, once for all, above the narrow interests of routine life and the mental strain which those interests involve. It is not suggested by this that art experience will not leave its good influence behind. All that is meant is that, whatever may be the nature and the extent of that influence, the experience itself, with the features that make it comparable to the ideal state, disappears after a time.

Secondly, art may prove so seductive to man that, in his zest for the pleasure it brings, he may grow negligent of his obligations to fellow-men. That is the moral, for instance, of Tennyson's *Palace of Art*. In it, as is well known, the poet describes a gifted soul as building for itself a fine and spacious mansion amidst magnificent surroundings, but on the summit of a hill far away from the common people. After ornamenting it with artistic works of great beauty and splendour, it enters the happy abode saying to itself, 'All these are mine; and let the world have peace or wars, it is one to me'. This self-complacent attitude, not doubt, does not continue very long, for the soul, which has thus isolated itself from others grows penitent of its pride and unsocial behaviour and at last steps down from its lofty position to join the common life and share its sorrows and its joys. But the poem makes it clear that there is nothing in aesthetic experience itself to guarantee against a life of self-centred satisfaction.

The ideal state will never be thus divorced from sympathy for fellow beings because, on the Indian view, it cannot be attained by any one who has not learnt to render loving service to others as the result of a thorough training in social morality. The *Kaṭha Upaniṣad* (I. ii. 24), for instance, is emphatic in stating that no one who has not overcome selfishness will ever reach the goal of life.

Lastly, the impersonal joy of art experience is induced artificially from outside, while that of the ideal state springs naturally from within. A few words are, perhaps, necessary to explain how this distinction between them arises:

(1) We have already referred to the dependence of art experience on an external stimulus. We have now to remark that it results from the contemplation not of a real, but of an imaginative or a fictitious situation created by the artist. That situation is also self-complete, for art, as is well known, deals in wholes. A perfect work of art has, indeed, been compared to a monad, for it admits of neither additions nor subtractions. The unique experience which accompanies the witnessing of a drama, say, is conditioned by both these features. Its impersonal character is explained by the unreality of the incidents represented on the stage. A frightful object appearing there will not incline even the most timid in the audience to shrink from it; nor will an alluring one prompt even the most covetous to cast a wishful eye on it. The attitude of the spectator towards them is one of appreciation merely, and there is no suggestion of anything to be done. Similarly, its restful joy is to be traced to the perfect unity of the situation depicted which, when realised, so satisfies the yearning in man for complete comprehension, or for knowing whatever there is to know, that it allays, for the moment, all his doubts and discomposing thoughts.

(2) Now as regards the ideal state: As pointed out before, it can be attained by no one that has not successfully undergone a course of moral training. That, however, is only one of the qualifications for reaching it. There is another, *viz.*, the acquisition of philosophic knowledge or, more strictly, the realisation of the ultimate truth. The ideal state is therefore the result of a combined pursuit of the values of truth and of goodness; and a person who succeeds in that pursuit comes to possess a comprehensive view of reality as well as a spirit of complete unselfishness. The same two conditions being thus present here as in the case of art experience, he derives the same kind of detached joy directly from the real universe. But the noteworthy point here is that, as the one represents a stable conviction about the nature of the universe and the other a permanent transformation of character, the state becomes not merely an adventitious one like art experience, depending upon an outer stimulus, but a natural and necessary expression of an inner attitude of the soul.

We may summarise what has been set forth, so far, as follows: The experience of art, like that of the ideal condition, is an ultimate value, in the sense that it is sought for its own sake and not as a means to anything else. Like the ideal condition again, art experience is characterised by a unique kind of delight; and in this, it is superior to common experience. But as it does not last very long, it may, when it passes off in consequence of the art stimulus being withdrawn, be succeeded by routine life with all its strifes and perplexities. In the case of the ideal experience, on the other hand, no such lapse is conceivable for it arises once for all and is permanent. Again, art experience does not require as a necessary condition of its attainment either philosophic knowledge or moral worth. It can be brought into being, even in their absence, by the power which all true works of art possess. That aesthetic contemplation can lead to the same kind of exalted experience as that of the ideal state, without all the arduous discipline—moral as well as intellectual— required for the latter, may appear to be an excellence of it. In a sense, no doubt, it is; and an old Indian art critic has declared, with exultation, that the bliss of *mokṣa*, which the *yogin* has to strain himself for long to win, is no match for it. But we should remember that art experience is woefully fugitive, and that the enduring character of the satisfaction that attends the ideal experience more than compensates for all the trouble and the exertion involved in attaining it.

It is, of course, possible to deny that there is any such enduring experience at all. An ideal like *mokṣa*, it may be said, is nothing more than a glorified idea—'the type of the perfect' in our mind which can never be actualised; it is because such experience is altogether beyond the reach of man that he has invented art as a means to escape from the cares and the responsibilities of ordinary life. This view assumes that the real neither is nor can ever become perfect, and that the ideal is always bound to remain unreal. It thus postulates a complete lack of harmony between the world of facts and the world of ideals. That is pessimism, pure and simple. It look upon life as 'a vale of tears', and regards art as nothing more than a hobby or a pastime to which man may turn for relief from the troubles of life. It may be that this doctrine of despair cannot be logically refuted. Yet the best thought all over the world is different. In any case, this pessimism has never commended itself to Indian thinkers; and many of them believe not only that it is possible to realise this goal, but that it can be reached even within the limits of the present life. According to them, art is much more than a means to secure for man a temporary escape from the imperfections of common life; it is an 'intimation' to him of the possibility of rising permanently above those imperfections. The limitations of the experience of art, to which we have alluded, do not affect the conclusion that it is of the same order as that of the ideal state; and we may well deduce from the fact of the one the feasibility of the other. Further, art experience is well adapted to arouse our interest in the ideal state by giving us foretaste of it, and thus to serve as a powerful incentive to the pursuit of that state. By provisionally fulfilling the need felt by man for restful joy, art experience may impel him to do his utmost to secure such joy finally.

5

Art Experience—2

OF THE INDIAN theories of art the most important is the one known as the Rasa theory. References to it are found in very early Sanskrit works, but it was not formulated and clearly expounded until the ninth century A.D.[1] In various directions, it marks an advance on the earlier theories and has virtually superseded them. In one respect, *viz.*, its conception of the aim of art, it is quite unique. The purpose of the present article is to explain the nature of this conception, and briefly to indicate wherein its uniqueness lies. Though the theory applies equally to all the fine arts, it has been particularly well-developed in relation to poetry and the drama; and we shall therefore consider it here mainly from that standpoint. But before we proceed to do so, it is desirable, for the sake of contrast, to make a reference to the general Indian view of poetry so far as it bears on the topic we are to consider.

I

There are two points of view from which the aim of poetry may be considered—one, of the poet, and the other, of the reader of poetry.[2] But for us, in explaining the distinctive feature of the

[1] This formulation is found in the *Dhvanyāloka* of Ānandavardhana. It was authoritatively commented upon in the tenth century A.D. by Abhinavagupta. We shall hereafter refer to this work as *DA.*, and our references will be to the first edition of it printed at Bombay in 1891.

[2] It is not meant by this that the two view-points necessarily differ in every respect.

view taken of it in the Rasa school, it is the latter that is more important. Let us therefore begin by asking the question: What is the use of poetry to its reader? The answer that is almost universally given to this question by Indian writers is pleasure (*prīti*).[3] It may have other uses also for him. For example, it may have some lesson or criticism of life to convey to him; but they are all more or less remote, unlike pleasure which is its immediate use[4] or value for him. But pleasure here is not to be taken in the abstract; rather, to judge from the explanation given of its nature in Indian works, it stands for a state of the self or a mode of experience of which it is a constant and conspicuous feature. Hence pleasure, by itself, does not constitute the whole of what is experienced at the time of poetic appreciation, but is only an aspect of it. The immediate value of poetry for the reader then is the attainment of this enjoyable experience and not mere pleasure. That is its primary use, and any other use it may have for him is a further good which poetry brings.

But pleasure, even when thus understood, is an end that is associated with many kinds of activities such, for example, as eating or bathing which none would place on the same level as poetry. It is therefore necessary to distinguish between the two. The distinction depends chiefly on the fact that, though art may eventually be based upon Nature, we are, in appreciating the objects it depicts, concerned more with their appearance than with their actual existence. In art, as it has been stated, 'we value the semblance above the reality'. So the artist selects only those among the features of the object to be depicted that are necessary for making his representation appear like it, and omits all the rest. A painter, for example, does not actually show us the thickness or depth of the things he paints, but yet succeeds in giving us an idea of their solidity. Art objects have consequently no place in the everyday world of space and time; and, owing to this lack of spatio-temporal position or physical status, the question

[3] See, e.g. Vāmana's *Kāvyālaṁkāra-sūtra*, I. i. 5.

[4] Cf. the term *sadyaḥ* ('instantly') used in describing the aim of poetry in *Kāvya-prakāśa* (Bombay Sanskrit Series), p. 8: *sadyaḥ paranirvṛti*. This work will be referred to as *KP*., hereafter.

of reality does not apply to them. This does not mean that they are unreal; it only means that the distinction of existence and non-existence does not arise at all in their case.[5]

But we should not think that these objects may therefore be of no interest to the reader. They have their own attraction for him, because a certain element of novelty enters into their representation. We have stated that the artist selects those features of the object he deals with which will make it retain its resemblance to the real. But that is not the whole truth, for he has also recourse often to fresh invention. Thus an Indian poet, in referring to the appearance of the earth on a moonlit night, represents it as 'carved out of ivory'. Almost all the writers on poetics lay down that *pratibhāna*, which may be rendered in English as 'creative fancy', is an indispensable condition of genuine poetry. It is 'the seed of poetry' (*kavitva-bīja*) according to them. But the Sanskrit word further connotes that the object so fancied is experienced *as if* it is being actually perceived—'like a globular fruit', it is said, 'placed on the palm of one's own hand'. But such invention does not mean the introduction of new features for their own sake. They are not merely pleasant fictions. When a poet, for instance, pictures fairies as dwelling in flowers or a cloud as carrying a message of love, he does so in strict conformity to the total imaginative vision which has inspired him to the creation of the particular work of art. The art object is thus much more than an appearance of the actual. It involves a good deal of mental construction and far surpasses in quality its counterpart in Nature.[6] In other words, the poet idealises the objects in depicting them; and it is in this process that they are raised to the level of art and acquire aesthetic significance and, though not real, come to be of interest to the reader.

As a result of their idealised character, art objects lose their

[5] Cf. *KP*., pp. 102–3, where this point is illustrated by the example of a 'painted horse' (*citra-turaga*).

[6] The following anecdote narrated about a famous painter of modern times brings out this feature very well. When the artist had painted a sunset, somebody said to him, 'I never saw a sunset like that'; and he replied, 'Don't you wish you could?'

appeal to the egoistic or practical self and appear the same to all. That is, art appreciation is indifferent not only to the distinction between the real and the unreal, but also to that between desire and aversion. They become impersonal in their appeal, and therefore enjoyable in and for themselves.[7] It is the complete detachment with which, in consequence, we view them, that makes our attitude then one of pure contemplation. But we must be careful to remember that by describing this attitude as contemplative, we do not mean that it is passive and excludes all activity. The very fact that it is an *appreciative* attitude implies that it is active. The belief that it is passive is the result of mistaking the disinterested for what is totally lacking in interest. But, as we have seen, the art object has its own interest to the spectator; and, so long as his mind is under the selective control of interest, it can by no means be regarded as passive. All that is meant by saying that the art object makes no appeal to the practical self is that our attention then is confined wholly to that object, and that it is not diverted therefrom by any thought of an ulterior use to which it may be put.

This transcendence of the egoistic self in the contemplation of art profoundly alters the nature of the pleasure derived from it. Being altogether divorced from reference to personal interests, one's own or that of others', art experience is free from all the limitations of common pleasure, due to the prejudices of everyday life such as narrow attachment and envy. In a word, the contemplation being disinterested, the pleasure which it yields will be absolutely pure. That is the significance of its description by Indian writers as 'higher pleasure' (*para-nirvṛti*).[8] And art will yield such pleasure, it should be observed, not only

[7] Cf. *KP.*, p. 107. This does not, however, mean that the response to them will be the same in the case of all. It will certainly vary, but only according to the aesthetic sensibilities of particular individuals and not according to their other personal peculiarities.

[8] See note 4 above on p. 34. Cf. the explanation of *prīti* as *alaulika-camatkāra* in *DA.*, p. 203 (com.). In view of this higher character, it would be better to substitute for it a word like 'joy' or 'delight'. But for the sake of uniformity, we shall generally use the word 'pleasure' itself.

when its subject-matter is pleasant, but even when it is not, as in a tragedy with its representation of unusual suffering and irremediable disaster. The facts poetised may, as parts of the actual world, be the source of pain as well as pleasure; but, when they are contemplated in their idealised form, they should necessarily give rise only to the latter. It is for this reason that pleasure is represented in Indian works as the *sole* aim of all art.[9] It means that the spectator, in appreciating art, rises above the duality of pain and pleasure as commonly known, and experiences pure joy. Here we see the differentia of poetic pleasure or, more generally, aesthetic delight.

II

The Rasa school agrees with the above conception of the poetic aim, but it distinguishes between two forms of it; and, since the distinction depends upon the view which the school takes of the theme of poetry, we have first to indicate the nature of that view. The theme of poetry, according to the general Indian theory, may be anything. One of the oldest writers on poetics in Sanskrit remarks that there is nothing in the realm of being or in that of thought which does not serve the poet's purpose.[10] Nor is any distinction made there between one topic and another as regards fitness for poetic treatment. One subject is as good as another, and there is none on which a fine poem might not be written. The Rasa school also admits the suitability of all themes for poetic treatment, but it divides them into two classes—one comprising those that are *dominated* by some emotion, particularly an elemental one like love or pathos, and the other all the remaining ones; and it holds that, for the purpose of poetic treatment, the first is superior to the second.[11] The exact significance of this bifurcation of themes will become clear as we proceed. For the

[9] *KP*., i. 1 (p. 2): (*hlādaikamayī*). Since no pleasure, as commonly known, answers to this description, it is not a hedonistic view of art, in the accepted sense, that we have here.

[10] Bhāmaha's *Kāvyālaṁkāra*, v. 4.

[11] *DA*., p. 28; pp. 20–7 (com.).

present, it will suffice to say that there are two types or order of poetry, according to this school, one dealing with 'emotional situations' in life, as we may describe them, and the other,[12] dealing with the other situations in life or with objects of external nature; and that the latter is reckoned as relatively inferior poetry. It is in justifying this discrimination that the Rasa school makes the differentiation in the purpose of poetry to which we have just referred. But before attempting to explain it, it is desirable to draw attention to one or two important points concerning emotional situations regarded as the theme of poetry.

A poem of the higher type, we have stated, depicts a situation which is predominantly emotional. This emphasis on the emotional character of the theme may lead one to suppose that the type resembles lyrical poetry, as distinguished (say) from the epic and the drama. The expression 'lyrical poetry' does not seem to have any very definite significance. But if, as implied by common usage, it stands for a particular class of poetry and signifies the expression by the poet of his own feelings,[13] we must say that, on neither of these considerations, is the above supposition correct:

In the first place, emotional situations may here to be the chief theme of *any* kind of poetry. In fact, their importance is discussed in the works of the school, particularly with reference to the drama; and the adoption of such a method is fully supported by the facts of India's literary history. Thus it is a situation of love that is dramatised by Kālidāsa in his famous play the *Śākuntala*; and, in the case of the equally famous play of Bhavabhūti, the *Uttara-rāma-carita* which treats of the desertion of Sītā by her royal husband, it is one of deep pathos. It is not merely dramas that may choose such topics for treatment; even extensive epics are not precluded from doing so. Thus the emotional element serves here as the basis for contrasting different *grades*,

[12] This class is further divided in a twofold way, but the division is not of importance for us here.

[13] Cf. 'Lyric poetry is the expression by the poet of his own feelings': Ruskin.

rather than different *forms* of poetry. We may adopt any classification of it we like. Every one of the resulting classes, according to the present view, will comprise two grades of poetry—one the higher, in which the theme is predominantly emotional, and the other the lower, in which it is not so.

In the next place, the poet's own feeling, according to the Rasa view, is *never* the theme of poetry. This point is usually explained by reference to the episode narrated in the beginning of the *Rāmāyaṇa* about the birth of Sanskrit classical poetry. The details of the episode are attractive enough to bear repetition, and they are briefly as follows: On a certain day, in a beautiful forest bordering on his hermitage, Vālmīki, the future author of the epic, it is said, chanced to witness a fowler killing one of a pair of lovely birds that were disporting themselves on the branch of a tree. The evil-minded fowler had singled out the male bird, and had brought it down at one stroke. Seeing it lie dead on the ground, all bathed in blood, its companion began to wail in plaintive tones. The soft-hearted sage was moved intensely by the sight; and he burst into song which was full of pathos and which, according to tradition, became the prelude to the composition of the first great epic in Sanskrit.

The poetic utterance is apt to be viewed as the expression of the sage's sorrow at the sight he witnessed; but writers of the Rasa school point out that it cannot really be so,[14] for the utterance of personal feeling would be quite different. It is hardly natural, they say, for one that is tormented by grief to play the poet.[15] The sage is not preoccupied with his own immediate reaction to what he saw, but with something else, *viz*., the objective

[14] *Na tu muneḥ śoka iti mantavyam*: *DA*., pp. 27–8 (com.).

[15] [In another paper called 'The Idea of Rasa' which was not published and which seems to be an earlier and shorter version of the present one, Prof. Hiriyanna has, at this place, the following footnote: 'This should not be taken to mean the elimination of all lyric poetry which, as ordinarily understood, gives expression to the poet's own feeling. It may well do so; only we have to look upon that feeling also as treated *objectively* by him in it. Cf. Wordsworth's saying, "Poetry springs from emotion recollected" (and, we should add, "sublimated") "in tranquility".'—Ed.]

scene itself. He is less concerned with his own feelings than with what has stirred them, and the song gives expression to the poignancy of the latter. But, as in the case of other poetic themes, it is not the emotional situation as it actually was (*laukika*) that is represented in it. That would by no means constitute art. It is the situation as it is in the poet's vision,[16] or as it has been transfigured by his sensitive nature and imaginative power (*alaukika*). In other words, the situation is idealised. Absorption in such a situation, for the reason already set forth, means transcending the tensions of ordinary life, and thereby attaining a unique form of experience. It is when the poet is fully under the spell of such experience that he spontaneously expresses[17] himself in the form of poetry.

III

To explain now the nature of the differentiation which the Rasa school makes in the aim of poetry: We have stated that poems may be of two kinds—one with an emotional theme and the other in which the theme is different, like (say) natural scenery:

(1) In the latter, there are the words of the poem; and the thoughts and images which they convey[18] form its essential content. It is the disinterested contemplation of them that gives rise to the joy of poetry. This contemplation, as a mental state, involves a subjective as well as an objective factor; and it is the total absorption in the objective factor, forgetting the subjective, that constitutes poetic experience here.

(2) But the case is altogether different in the other type of poetry. For the central feature of the situation to be portrayed in

[16] Indian writers describe this as 'in the poem' (*kāvya-gata*) to distinguish it from the fact poetised, which is outside it. See *DA*., p. 56 (com.).

[17] *Yāvat pūrṇo na caitena tāvan naiva vamaty amum*: *DA*., p. 27 (com.).

[18] It is not meant that words in a poem always or necessarily form only the medium of conveying thoughts or images. They may, and often do contribute directly to the beauty of the poem. We are overlooking that point since our purpose here is to bring out the distinction in aim in the case of the two types of poetry we are considering, and not to explain the nature of either completely.

it is an emotion; and no emotion is, in its essence, directly describable. The poet cannot therefore communicate it, as he can a thought or image.[19] He can only suggest it[20] to the reader, who has already had personal experience of it (for it cannot be made known to any other), by delineating its causes and consequences or, in other words, the objects that prompt it and the reactions which they provoke. That is, the emotional aspect of the situation can be indicated only in an indirect or mediate sense, the media being the thoughts and images, as conveyed by the poet's words, of the objective constituents of that situation. Thus what, by themselves, form the content in the other type of poetry here become the means to its suggestion. They accordingly occupy a place here similar to the one occupied by words there;[21] and the final aesthetic fact in this type of poetry thereby comes to be, not thoughts and images as in the other, but the emotional mood which they help to induce in the reader. Now, as an emotion is a phase of our own being and not a presentation, this mood cannot be *contemplated*, but can only be *lived through*;[22] and it is this inner process of experiencing that is the ultimate meaning or aim in this type of poetry. There is a presentational element involved in this case also, as certainly as there is in the other, and it has, of course, its own poetic quality of beauty, if we like to put it so; but reduced, as it becomes here, to merely a condition

[19] The use of words like 'love' and 'anger' may convey to a person, who knows their meaning, an idea of the corresponding emotion; but it will be only an *idea* of them, while what is meant here is a *felt* emotion. See *DA*., pp. 24–6.

[20] To use technical terms, it will necessarily be *vyaṅgya*. Thoughts and images also may be suggested; but they are, at the same time expressible and therefore *vācya* also.

[21] See *DA*., pp. 31–2, 190–1.

[22] The same may appear to hold good of the other phases of mind also, but it does not. To consider the case of 'thought', the only one of them that has a bearing on our subject (see next note): According to the Indian conception, the term 'thought' (jñāna) means 'what reveals' (*prakāśaka*); and thought, in this sense, is always intimately connected with 'what is revealed' by it (*prakāśya*), *viz*., the object. Hence the *process of thinking*, apart from reference to some presentation, is meaningless. When it has meaning, i.e. 'when it is considered along with the presentational element', it becomes expressible and can also be contemplated. Cf. *Arthenaiva viśeṣo his nirākāratayā dhiyām*.

of suggesting the emotion, it slides into the margin in our consciousness, instead of occupying the focus as it does there.[23]

Thus the experience for which poetic appreciation stands here is vastly different from that for which it does in the other type of poetry. It also connotes detached joy; but, while the other experience takes the form of contemplating the poetic object, this one takes the form entirely of an inward realisation. The distinction will become clear, if we consider one or two examples. Let us contrast the example, already cited, of imagining the moonlit earth as 'carved out of ivory', with the appreciation of Kālidāsa's *Cloud Messenger*, which depicts the forlorn state of a lover exiled from his home. In the former, there is plainly an external object in the focus of our attention; but in the latter, though it abounds in exquisite pictures of external nature, we have finally to look within in order to appreciate properly its ultimate meaning, *viz.*, the deep anguish of forced separation from the beloved. To take another pair of illustrations, let us compare Milton's description, in the *Nativity Hymn*, of the rising sun as 'in bed curtained with cloudy red' and as pillowing 'his chin upon an orient wave', and Tennyson's well-known lyric, *Break, break, break*, with its poignant lament for lost love, heightened by a knowledge of the difference of the world, as a whole, to the suffering of the individual. In the former, the reader is engrossed in an object outside himself; but, in the latter, he has to retreat, as it were, into his inner self to realise its final emotional import. Both varieties of experience, as being aesthetic, are marked by a temporary forgetting of the self. But while in one case, the objective factor is *integral* to the ultimate poetic experience; in the other, it is not so,[24] because it has, as we have seen, only a marginal significance. That is, the emotion is experienced here virtually by itself, and the experience may accordingly be said to

[23] Ordinarily an emotion, no doubt, is also directed upon some object; but here, as aesthetic activity is not practical in its usual sense, this element is lacking.

[24] Cf. *Rasādir artho hi sahaiva vācyenāvabhāsate*: *DA*., p. 67. See also pp. 182–7.

transcend, in a sense, the subject-object relation, and therefore to be of a higher order[25] than the mere contemplation of the other kind of poetry. It is this higher experience, that is called 'Rasa'.

The word 'Rasa' primarily means 'taste' or 'savour', such as sweetness; and, by a metaphorical extension, it has been applied to the type of experience referred to above. The point of the metaphor is that, as in the case of a taste like sweetness, there is no knowing of Rasa apart from directly experiencing it.[26] This experience, in addition to having its own affective tone or feeling of pleasure which is common to all aesthetic appreciation, is, as we know, predominantly emotional; and it is the latter feature, *viz.*, the predominance of its emotional quality, that distinguishes it from the experience derivable from the other type of poetry, dealing with a subject like natural scenery. It naturally differs according to the specific kind of emotion portrayed—love, pathos, fear, wonder and the like; and, on the basis of this internal difference, Rasa experience is ordinarily divided into eight or nine kinds. But it is not necessary for our present purpose to enter into these details. Besides, Rasa is, in its intrinsic nature, but *one* according to the best authorities;[27] and its so-called varieties are only different forms of it, due to a difference in their respective psychological determinants. In its fundamental character, it signifies a mood of emotional exaltation which, on the ground of what has been stated so far, may be characterised as quite unique.

It is necessary to dwell further on the nature of this experience, if what is meant by Rasa is to be properly understood. We have shown that when a poet treats of an emotional theme, he never depicts his own feeling, but only that which distinguishes the objective situation occasioning that feeling. This should not be taken to mean that it is the awareness (to revert to our earlier

[25] It will be noticed that, in thus ascribing a superior status to Rasa experience, the value of neither the subjective nor the objective factor is denied, since the need for it of personal experience (remotely) and of appropriate objective accompaniments (externally) is fully recognised.

[26] Cf. *āsvādyamānatā-prāṇatayā bhānti*: *DA*., p. 24 (com.).

[27] Cf. *Abhinava-bhāratī*, I, pp. 273–4, 293.

illustration) of the bird's sorrow at the loss of its mate, even in its idealised form, which constitutes Rasa experience.[28] As already implied, it consists in an ideal revival (*udbo-dhana*) in the reader's mind of a like emotion which, being elemental by hypothesis, may be expected to lie latent in all. Being a revival, it necessarily goes back to his past experience; but it is, at the same time, very much more than a reminiscence. In particular, the emotional situation, owing to the profound transformation which it undergoes in the process of poetic treatment, will throw a new light on that experience, and reveal its deeper significance for life as, for instance, in the case of love, in Kālidāsa's *Śākuntala*, which appears first as the manifestation of a natural impulse but is transformed before the play concludes into what has been descried as 'a spiritual welding of hearts'. To realise such significance fully, the reader's own efforts become necessary in the way of imaginatively reproducing in his mind the whole situation as it has been depicted by the poet. Rasa experience is thus the outcome more of reconstruction than of remembrance. The whole theory is based on the recognition of an affinity of nature between the poet and the reader of poetry; and, on the basis of this affinity, it is explained that appreciation of poetry is essentially the same as the creation of it.[29] The need for presupposing past experience arises from the peculiar nature of emotion, to which we have already drawn attention, *viz.*, its essential privacy owing to which it remains opaque, as it were, to all those who have not personally felt it. But past experience serves merely as the centre round which the reconstruction takes place; and, in this reconstructed form, it is anything but personal.[30]

The point to be specially noticed here is that emotions are not *communicated* by the poet to the reader, as it is often assumed.[31] In fact, they *cannot* be communicated according to the present theory. All that the poet can do is to awaken in him an emotion

[28] *DA.*, pp. 56–7 (com.).

[29] *Nāyakasya kaveḥ srotuḥ samānonubhavaḥ*. *DA.*, p. 20 (com.). Cf. 'To listen to a harmony is to commune with its composer'.

[30] *Tat-kāla-vigalita-parimita-pramātṛ-bhāva*: *KP.*, p. 108.

[31] Cf. What has been described as the 'infection theory' of Tolstoy.

similar to the one he is depicting. Even this awakening, it should be noted, is not the result of any conscious purpose on the part of the poet. The spontaneous character of all poetic utterance precludes such a supposition. The poet is intent, not upon influencing the reader in this or that way, but upon giving expression, as best he can, to his unique experience. It is this expression, that is primary, and the kindling up or waking to life of the emotion in the mind of the reader is more in the nature of its consequence than the result of any set purpose behind it. The reader starts from the poet's expression; and, if he is competent, that is, if he is sufficiently sensitive and sympathetic, he succeeds in capturing for himself the experience which it embodies. The process whereby such ideal awakening takes place is described:[32] Briefly, the mind of the responsive reader first becomes attuned to the emotional situation portrayed (*hṛdaya-saṁvāda*), through one or more of the knowing touches which every good poem is sure to contain; is then absorbed in its portrayal (*tanmayībhavana*); and this absorption, in the deeper sense already explained, results in the aesthetic rapture of Rasa (*rasānubhava*).

If this type of poetry were identical with lyrical and with short poems, we might have a relatively simple emotion as its characteristic feature. But when its scope is widened as here, the emotions involved may be very complex, indeed. In an epic, for example, practically all the familiar emotions are likely to appear at one stage or another; and, if they are not well co-ordinated, the aesthetic value of the poem will suffer. Hence the exponents of the Rasa view lay down that the treatment of the theme by the poet should be such as to secure the unity of the different emotions suggested—a unity which, they insist, is as important a canon of poetic composition here, as the unity of action is admitted to be in the case of all poetry.[33] Only a single emotion should be represented in a poem as dominant on the whole; and its progressive development from the moment of its emergence to its natural culmination should be methodically delineated. Its

[32] See, e.g. *DA.*, pp. 11, 15, 24 and 27 (com.).
[33] *DA.*, pp. 170–1.

many and varied manifestations should be properly related to it, so that its portrayal may become internally coherent. Where other emotions, not altogether incompatible with it, enter the situation, they should all be synthetically related to it. Everything else also, like the construction of the plot, the interludes, characterisation and the poetic imagery in which the artist clothes his ideas should be oriented towards the ruling emotion. Even the diction and the other refinements of style must be appropriate to its nature. In one word, fitness (*aucitya*) of everything that has any bearing on it is the life-breath of Rasa.[34] This topic occupies considerable space in the works of the school; but, in view of its uniform recognition of the spontaneity of all poetic utterance, the rules formulated in this connection are to be looked upon more as aids in appraising the worth of a poem of this type than as restraints placed upon the freedom of the poet.

But the intrinsic worth of a poem is not all that is needed for its true appreciation. The reader also should be properly equipped for it. No doubt, the emotion depicted in this type of poetry is elemental, and therefore familiar to all. But that only signifies the universality of its appeal. It means that nobody is excluded from appreciating it, merely by virtue of its theme. The reader, in addition to possessing a general artistic aptitude specially qualified, if he is to appraise and enjoy a poem of the present type.[35] These qualifications are compendiously indicated by saying that he should be a *sa-hṛdaya*,[36] a word which cannot easily be rendered in English. It literally means 'one of similar heart', and may be taken to signify a person whose insight into the nature of poetry is, in point of depth, next only to that of the poet. In the absence of adequate equipment, he may lose sight of the Rasa aspect and get absorbed in the objective details portrayed by the poet which also, as we said, have a poetic qualify of their own. We would then be preferring the externals of true poetry to its essence; or, as Indian critics put it, he would mistake the

[34] *DA*., p. 145.
[35] *DA*., pp. 18–19 (com.).
[36] *DA*., p. 11 (com.).

'body' (*śarīra*) of poetry for its 'soul' (*ātman*).[37] To cite a parallel from another of the fine arts, he will be like a person who, in looking on a statue of Buddha in meditative posture, remains satisfied with admiring the beauty, naturalness and proportion of its outward features, but fails to realise the ideal of serenity and calm depicted there, which constitutes its ultimate meaning. It is on this basis, *viz.*, that it is not merely the intrinsic excellence of a poem that is required for attaining Rasa experience but also a special capacity for it in the reader, that the present school explains how, though great poets like Kālidāsa have tacitly endorsed the Rasa view by the place of supremacy they have given to emotion in their best works, it took so long for theorists to discover that they had done so.

Such, in brief outline, is the Rasa view advocated by what is known as the 'later' (*navīna*) school of art critics in India, as distinguished from the 'earlier' (*prācīna*). We have already drawn attention to one or two important points in the Rasa theory, in which it differs from the generality of aesthetic views. For example, it rejects the very common view that a poet may, and often does, give expression to his own feelings in poetry. Here is another point which is far more important, *viz.*, the discovery that there is an order of poetry which requires a deeper form of appreciation and yields a higher kind of aesthetic experience than is ordinarily acknowledged; and in this discovery, we may say, consists one of the chief contributions of India to the general philosophy of art.

[37] *DA.*, p. 13 (com.).

6

Indian Aesthetics—2

INTRODUCTORY

IT IS USUAL for every prominent philosopher in the West to regard the question of beauty as a part of the problem he is attempting to solve. Hence aesthetics has come to be recognised there as a regular part of philosophy. The intrinsic relation implied in this between aesthetics and philosophy is not denied in India; but the former of these studies is carried on by a distinct class of thinkers—*ālaṁkārikas*, as they are called or literary critics—who are not, generally speaking, professional philosophers. This separation of aesthetic problems, in the matter of investigation, from those of general philosophy may at first sight appear not only strange but also defective; a little reflection, however, will show that it is not really so. Before explaining this point, however, it is necessary to state that when we say that Indian philosophers have not troubled themselves with questions of beauty, what is meant is only that they do not deal with beauty in art and not also beauty in nature. The latter is certainly included; but, while it is explicit in some systems, it is only implicit in others. The exact view which they hold in this respect will become clear as we proceed. As regards their neglect of beauty in art, the reason is that its pursuit cannot, according to them, directly minister to the attainment of the final goal of life, which is the prime concern of Indian philosophers. Perhaps some among them thought that its pursuit might even tend to lead man away from that goal, in which case their attitude towards art would be like that of Plato towards the same.

So far from being a defect, the separation of aesthetics in this sense from general philosophy has many positive advantages. It has thereby been able to get rid of the constraint which particular types of metaphysical thought may impose upon it. When a philosopher holds a particular view of reality, he is bound to square his theory of art, if he formulates one, with it; and the consequence is that we have as many theories of art in the West as there are theories of reality. This cannot be helped in the case of beauty in nature, but there is no reason for acquiescing in such diversity of views in a theory of art. That is the view of Indian aestheticians. Thus the postulation by Indian aestheticians of what is called *vyaṅgyārtha*, which is not only not recognised by any school of philosophy but is definitely opposed, shows the freedom with which aesthetic investigation has been carried on in India.[1] They have succeeded in this in evolving a theory of meaning which, as we shall try to point out, certainly sheds new light on the nature of art. Where it is not necessary to devise such a new theory, Indian aestheticians select one or other of the views held by the philosophic schools according to the needs of the case. Such eclecticism results in a more detached view (from the aesthetic standpoint) than would be the case if a particular philosophic point of view were adopted in its entirety. This does not, however, mean that there is a dull uniformity in the Indian theory of art. There is as much diversity in it as in any Western treatment of the subject; but the important point is that the diversity is based upon purely artistic considerations and is therefore more genuine.

There is another reason to support the Indian practice. Reality, as represented in art, as is generally admitted, is a unity in diversity, so that there is no room for any divergence of opinion in regard to it, so far as art is concerned. The aim of art is not to

[1] See Jayaratha's commentary on Ruyyaka's *Alaṁkārasarvasva*, p. 10, (Nir. S. Pr.).

discover the nature of reality but to secure for us the highest experience of life. It does not pronounce any final opinion on the tenability or otherwise of the view of reality it thus uses. In other words, aesthetics, unlike ethics for instance, is alogical. While it is closely connected with psychology it regards logic, or more properly epistemology, as irrelevant to its purpose. Art is a short cut to the ultimate value of life, by-passing logic. Even supposing it is not admitted that reality, as represented in art, is necessarily a unity in diversity, the view of reality that may be accepted in its stead does not matter, for it is to serve but as the medium through which the value is realised, art being concerned less with facts than with values.

1. Nature and Art

We have distinguished nature from art. The question will naturally arise here whether there is any need for seeking beauty in art, if it is found in nature. As G. E. Moore has stated in his *Principia Ethica*, when other things are the same, beauty which is found in actual objects is decidedly better than that in imaginary ones. It is therefore necessary to point out why art is necessary, though in certain respects the beauty which it presents may be inferior to that in nature. As regards the latter, two views are possible.

(i) We may hold, with the idealists, that nature as a whole is beautiful, but that when it is looked at in parts, it may or may not be so. That is, though nature may, in reality, be beautiful, there may appear ugliness in it when we take a partial view of it as, ordinarily speaking, we are bound to do. This means that, though in the case of those few who can take a synoptic view of nature, art may be superfluous, it is not so in the case of the many. As an old Vedāntic stanza has it, it is only 'when man has overcome selfishness and realised the highest truth, he will be in rapt ecstasy wherever he may turn', for he sees the glory of Being everywhere. Till then therefore he can have an experience of complete beauty only in art. Further, even as regards the parts that appear beautiful in nature, there is no certainty that they will continue to be so for long. For there may come to be a change in our attitude towards them, when their appeal will become non-aesthetic. Or the situations in nature may themselves so change in course of time that they will cease to appear beautiful. Hence it is that we require the creations of art which are not subject to these defects—a change in the presentations of nature or in our attitude towards them. This is the need for art according to the idealistic view of nature.

(ii) The second view of nature is that though it may be beautiful, that feature is inevitably associated with ugliness and that the latter element cannot be eliminated from it without, at the same time, eliminating the former also. According to this pessimistic view, art becomes even more necessary. In fact, it is the *sole* means, in this view, of satisfying the quest for unmixed joy which somehow actuates all men or, to state the same otherwise, the need for escaping from the struggles and perplexities of everyday life.

Whatever the worth of these two metaphysical theories in themselves may be, the point that is important for us now is that there is a need for art in either case. To state this need in terms applicable to both the views, it is the presence, on the one hand, of evil in life and, on the other, of an ideal within us that has led to the invention of art. Here we may observe, in passing, we have another instance of Indian aesthetics transcending the differences that characterise the metaphysical schools. Art is a device for the provisional attainment of the final ideal of life, whether or not we look forward to a state which eventually renders it superfluous.[2]

2. Art Experience

The aim of art is implicit in what we have said so far. It is to secure for man a unique form of experience which, according to one view, can never be attained in actual life and, according to

[2] There is an ultimate ideal according to the second view also; but it is a state transcending joy as well as suffering. Positivistically speaking, this means that man may cultivate detach-ment to such an extent that he will ignore nature altogether. But there is nothing resembling aesthetic pleasure then, unless we understand the aesthetic end itself in an uncommon way.

the other, can be attained only when self-perfection is achieved. But either way, it is an ultimate value in the sense that it is sought for its own sake and not as a means to anything else.[3] The characteristics of this art experience are two:

(1) The first is unselfishness. It is true that all or nearly all men, in virtue of their social nature, show more or less of unselfishness in their behaviour; but it may be the result of habit or of prudential, and therefore eventually of selfish, considerations. Such outward unselfishness is not what is meant here. Even when it is spontaneous and therefore quite genuine, it is not complete. The selfishness signified by art experience, on the other hand, is not only spontaneous but also complete. Man grows so unselfish then that he becomes virtually unconscious of his private self. This is the meaning of saying that art experience consists in the disinterested contemplation of beauty. The intrusion of any personal aim is sure to vitiate it, and make the pursuit of art unsuccessful.

(2) The second characteristic, which is probably a consequence of the first, is that it yields a kind of joy which is pure and untainted by even the least pain. This is a further indication of the transcendental character of art experience; and it shows that the aesthetic attitude stands higher than that of common or everyday life which is invariably characterised by more or less of mental tension.

On account of these excellences, art experience is regarded as identifiable with the ultimate goal of life as it is conceived by the idealists. When we take the ideal of life, as it is conceived by others, art experience affords the same escape from worldly concerns as that ideal, when attained, does; but it also does more for, while the latter does not represent a state of supreme joy, the former does. According to both, it is one of the only two such values recognised by Indians—*ātmānanda* and *rasānubhava*.

[3] Self-realisation in Advaita is value-realisation, for the Self is the ultimate value.

The Content of Art

But what is the means whereby the artist is able to secure for us such experience? All art is a blend of form and content; and it is through certain excellences characterising either, that he succeeds in inducing in us the artistic attitude. In the case of poetry, for example, the content is constituted by the figurative ideas and sentiments it expresses; and the form, by the musical language through which they find expression. Of these, the form varies much from one art to another; and it is also technical. We shall not refer to it here at any length, and shall confine our attention mainly to the content. We shall only observe, in passing, that the legitimate function of form is to subserve the content; and if it assumes greater importance, the work in which it does so marks a lapse from the best type of art.

The content of art may be defined generally as the meaning which it expresses. The excellences that may characterise it are many, and they have been classified in various ways. But these details, while they are undoubtedly helpful in indicating to us their character in a concrete manner, can never be exhaustively enumerated. As one Indian literary critic observes,[4] they can only be indicated generally. This general character of the content of art is that it must be drawn from actual life, but that it should also be judiciously idealised. The purpose of the idealisation is two-fold: In the first place, it is that, having its source in the artist's imagination, it may appeal to the same faculty in the spectator and not to his intellect merely. In the second place, it is that the particular things of common experience may thereby be transformed into general ones, and thus readily induce a detached attitude in the spectator which, as we have pointed out, is a salient feature of all art experience. But it is necessary to add that the things represented in art will not become false or fictitious through such idealisation. For a spectator to mistake them for real objects, as we do in illusions, will be to lapse from the truly aesthetic attitude, because he will then cease to remain

[4] Cf. *Vāgabhaṭālaṁkāra*, p. 77.

detached. But at the same time, they cannot be viewed as unreal or false because then they will cease to interest him. Thus the things depicted in art assume a unique character which the spectator can describe as neither real nor unreal. In brief, we do not take a logical view of them. We neither believe nor disbelieve in their reality. We merely entertain them.[5]

This is the general view of the content of art which is prevalent everywhere. Indian aestheticians also held the same opinion for a long time; but a profound change in this respect, the germs of which seem to have been there all along, was introduced about the ninth century A.D. The change was to look upon what had so far been regarded as the content of art, *viz.*, the meaning also as only the outer vesture of art and to take emotion as its true content.[6] When the meaning in general was regarded as the content, it might be emotion or might not be; but now it is laid down that it should be only emotion. We have stated that the appeal of art should be to the imagination; and imagination always implies the presence of emotion in some degree or other. But it is not this emotion that we should think of now. It is the emotional character of the situation depicted by the artist that constitutes the true content of art, and the type of experience to which it gives rise in the spectator is called *rasa*. A consequence of this change in the idea of the content of art was to deny that the expressed meaning can have any excellences of its own and to assert that, like the form, it also has them only in relation to the emotion which it is intended to subserve. The excellences of meaning may be the very best, according to earlier standards; but yet they may produce the exact opposite of artistic feeling in the spectator, if they are out of harmony with the emotion depicted. This rightly introduces a relativistic view into art criticism; and neither form nor meaning was thenceforward regarded as beautiful in itself. The standards by which they were judged remained more or less the same, but they ceased to be taken as absolute.

We may point out before concluding this topic that the earlier view of art as consisting in the excellences characterising its

[5] Cf. 'Poetic Truth'.

[6] [Poetry was] brought nearer music thereby.

form and meaning was not abandoned. That view also was retained; but works answering to that description came to be assigned an inferior status. It is designated *citra*, a term which, in all probability signifies that its merit lies more in skill which appeals to our intellect rather than in affecting our life or soul.

The Method of Art

Now emotions cannot be directly communicated. We can, of course, talk of (say) love or fear; but these words, when used by themselves, merely convey the idea of the corresponding feeling and do not communicate it to the listener. Such communication of it is possible only through a proper portrayal of select aspects of its causes and consequences. That is, the artist is obliged, if he is to succeed in what is his foremost aim, to adopt an indirect method in dealing with his material. This method is called *dhvani*; and secondarily, the work of art also, which is characterised by it, is designated by the same term. It had always been recognised as important for the artist, but only as one of those at his disposal for coveying the appropriate sentiment to the spectator. We may instance, as illustrating this point, *alaṁkāras* like *paryāyokta* and *samāsokti*, which are mentioned in the earliest *alaṁkāra* works. The discovery that was made later was that it was the *sole* method of the best type of art. This we may add, was the direct consequence of recognising *rasa* to be the aim *par excellence* of the artist. The method of art is thus as unique as its aim.

The method of *dhvani* has naturally been extended to other spheres of art where direct communication is possible, *viz.*, *alaṁkāras*; and has led to a preference being shown to them when they are indirectly suggested, instead of being directly expressed. Owing, however, to the intimate connection between imagination on which *alaṁkāras* are chiefly based and emotion on which *rasa* is, the difference between them is not always quite definite. The one may easily pass into another. Hence the decision in any particular case, depends upon the view one takes of it; and it accordingly becomes personal, illustrating the well-known saying that tastes differ. Another extension of this theory of *dhvani* is to those poetic representations, which can be regarded neither as *rasa* nor as *alaṁkāra* and are therefore indefinitely designated as *vastu*. The innovation thus introduced by the *dhvani* canon here, like that in the case of *alaṁkāras*, we may observe, is more in rearranging conclusions that had already been reached than in making any new additions. The above statements enable us to divide the subject of first-rate art in a triple way. It may be emotion, when the resulting experience is called *rasa-dhvani*; it may be any other imaginative situation, in which case it will be *alaṁkāradhvani*; or it may be a matter-of-fact representation, in which case it will be *vastu-dhvani*.

The discovery that the *dhvani* method is the secret of true art furnishes another instance of what we described above as the alogical character of art. The conclusions suggested by this method vary according to the persons concerned and the contexts to which they belong, although the premises given are the same. At best, the mental process involved resembles analogical reasoning. Some of the erroneous views current before the method of *dhvani* was formulated or after are due to mistaking the method of art to be logical. Thus Mahima Bhaṭṭa tried to make out that the process involved in the so-called *dhvani* was nothing but inferential; and others like Mukula Bhaṭṭa represented the secondary senses of words as derived through the *pramāṇa* known as *arthāpatti*. Both forgot that the *dhvani* lacks the element of necessity, which is essential to what is strictly a logical process.

3. Art and Morality

We have referred to two views of reality in explaining the need for art. Whichever of them we may adopt, the implication is the presence of evil in life. According to one of these views, evil is finally removable; according to the other also it is so, only its removal involves the removal of good as well along with it. Overlooking this distinction which is really irrelevant for art, we may ask what the bearing of art is on the problem of evil, which it thus implicitly postulates.[7]

[7] It is the problem of evil that gives rise to art as well as to philosophy.

It may appear that art cannot be unconnected with morality, since the experience which it yields is, as we have pointed out, essentially disinterested; and disinterestedness is the very root of all morality. It is therefore necessary to examine what precisely the significance of this attitude is. To begin with, the ethical attitude is more than one of mere detachment. It is essentially active; but activity is, from the very nature of the case, wholly excluded from art experience. Or to state the same otherwise, the ethical attitude is orientated towards some purpose, while the artistic is quite the reverse, its sole purpose being the transcendence of all purpose. It is an attitude of contemplation rather than of achievement. Even as regards the unselfishness, which it shares with the ethical attitude, there is a vital distinction. There are two points to be noted in connection with it. In the first place, the aesthetic attitude is induced by an external stimulus. When once it has arisen, it may be quite genuine; but we cannot overlook the fact that it is due to an external influence. Morality which springs from fear of punishment or hope of reward is really no morality at all. The unselfishness characterising the ethical attitude, on the other hand, springs from inside and is quite spontaneous. It is only when it is the result of an inner urge that it will be of an enduring influence on life. But this later feature is lacking in the case of the art attitude, which we chiefly owe to the power that all true works of art possess. That such an exalted attitude can be produced, without any arduous trouble on the part of the spectator, is indeed an excellence of it; but it is unfortunately fugitive. Sooner or later, it comes to an end for it cannot last longer than the outside stimulus which has evoked it. Even such short-lived experience may, through refining emotions, leave some good influence behind; but the point to be noted is that there is no guarantee that it will. In the second place, the disinterestedness of the aesthetic attitude marks a reaction to an imaginary situation and not to a real one. It results from the contemplation not of actual but fictitious situations created by the artist. Fiction facilitates detachment. The consequence of this again is unfavourable to true morality, whose proper sphere is actual life. Thus even though perfect selflessness may be a prominent mark of art experience, its influence on the moral side of man may be very little. When that experience ceases he may lapse into the former state of tension and perplexity, which has its source in a selfish outlook on life.

According to some, this is no defect at all; for art, they maintain, has nothing to do with morality and is ethically neutral. But if that is so, it ceases to be a human value; and its recognition of evil as a fat of life becomes virtually meaningless.[8] There has been much controversy in this respect among art critics; but if we take a comprehensive view of man's nature and his aims, it seems that art cannot be altogether divorced from morality.[9] Art is, no doubt, for its own sake. But, in the result, it should be more by being a criticism of life's values. This explains, for instance, the double standard of our judging a character appearing in a work of art. To take the case of Iago, as an example, we not only speak of him as a perfect creation of Shakespeare but also condemn him as wicked in the extreme. The practice of the best artists is our support here. And the close alliance, again, of art with religion in all countries and in all times appears to be for saving art from possible degeneration by its separation from morality.[10] Art, correctly conceived, cannot be merely a selfish escape from life; it must also influence life permanently or, at least, tend to do so. But the view that art is not connected with morality is not altogether baseless. The truth underlying it is that art has nothing *directly* to do with morality. It should influence character indirectly; and what is discountenanced is only direct instruction in that regard, for it will militate against the primary purpose of art which is to raise man above all strife and secure a form of unique joyful experience.[11]

[8] It would also then cease to appeal to the whole being of man which, as an ultimate value, it is expected to do.

[9] It would then amount to a selfish escape from the tedium of life—a view as blameworthy as pure asceticism is in ethics. Both are at bottom egoistic, being preoccupied with oneself and not caring in the least for society.

[10] The association of art with religion, in all probability, is primarily to make the latter attractive; but it has undoubtedly helped to prevent the former from deteriorating.

[11] In this sense, the following statement of Bhaṭṭa Nāyaka is correct: *Kavye rasayitā sarvo na boddhā na niyoga-bhāk.* [Quoted in *DA*. (com.), p. 12.]

When even the primary aim of art is to be attained indirectly, it is natural to ask: What is this indirect connection between art and morality? It cannot be due to the method of art, for fables and parables teach morality indirectly but are not art. It must be through the characters which it introduces or, what comes to the same thing, through the general significance of the plot, that art can exercise moral influence on the spectators.[12] The implied outlook of these characters on life and the world should be moral. 'That is a true poem', says an old Indian authority, 'which treats of the doings of the good and the great'. The best examples of this are to be found in the great epics of the *Rāmāyaṇa* and the *Mahābhārata* whose indirect influence on Indian men and women has all along been greater than that of any other single factor. In a work of art where no such characters are found, say, a lyric poem, it is the artist's outlook on what he portrays that counts. The conclusion to be drawn from this is that art should not have a moral *aim*, but most necessarily have a moral *view*, if it should fulfil its true purpose.[13] This is not to make art didactic, for morality does not form either its content or its purpose according to this view.

In addition to this general moral view, there may be some aspect of the moral idea dominating the conduct of the hero or of other characters, and be thus intimately woven into the structure of the plot.[14] It will then become an organic part of the content of art. A very good example of it is found in Bhavabhūti's drama, *Uttararāma-carita*. Here, as in any other great work of art, there is a general moral view pervading the whole piece. It includes not a single character which leads to any lapse from the high level that is expected in a play of which Rāma is the hero.

[12] It is not what the characters say that counts; but what they are and what they do.

[13] No artist will present characters like Iago as examples to be followed. But this negative attitude towards them is not enough. He should do his best to leave the impression on us that they are warnings.

[14] This is the meaning of Indian critics saying that any of the *puruṣārthas* may be the content of art. When either *artha* or *kāma* forms the content, a general moral view is expected to prevail; when *dharma* becomes the content, there is this additional emphasis on morality.

But over and above this, there is Rāma's sense of public duty (as interpreted by him, of course) and his determination that it should have priority over all private obligations, which forms the very pivot on which the whole of the story here dramatised turns.[15] Unlike the general moral view, this is in the foreground of the picture. But it must be added that it, in no way, encroaches upon the artistic function of the play which is to awaken in us the emotion of love—not as the source of all life's joy, but as leading to pathos which so often and so inexplicably comes in its wake. This emphasis on the importance of public duty may be the main lesson of the story. But the story is not the end in dramatic art; it is only a means to the communication to the spectators of the *rasa* in question.

That is, the creations of art must leave a moral influence on the spectator without his knowing that he is being so influenced. Though theoretically, the theme of art may be anything which has a basis in life, this additional requirement makes it necessary to restrict the scope of the artist's choice to the higher aspects of life. Otherwise, art not only ceases to exert any moral influence; it may turn out in the end to be a means of corrupting character and degrading ideals.

[15] There is no hesitation whatever before the dictate of reason that a ruler must put public good before private inclination and there is a majestic sadness in the banishment of Sītā as a consequence.

7

Art and Morality

BOTH ART AND morality spring from a sense of deficiency in the existing state of things. Morality represents an attempt to rectify that deficiency by actually changing the state, while art affords an escape from it by providing a world of ideal construction. If man were a perfect being placed in the midst of a perfect environment—social as well as natural—there would be little need for either art or morality.

But it may be asked whether all conscious activity does not have the same end, *viz.*, the rectification of or escape from some deficiency in a given situation. That is, no doubt, so; but there is one important difference in the case of art and morality. They signify an attitude of absolute disinterestedness. They imply that one and the same end may be pursued in two ways—with selfish inclination allowed to have its play or without it; and it is the preference of the latter to the former that differentiates art and morality from common activities. If we are working for an end, the activity becomes moral when that end is sought to the complete exclusion of selfish gain. Similarly, if we are contemplating a situation, the contemplation becomes aesthetic when we are so much overpowered by it that we forget ourselves. Whether art and morality signify anything more is a matter for us to consider later. For the present, it will suffice to observe that they imply not merely a consciousness of deficiency in a given situation but also a dissatisfaction with the way in which attempts[1]

[1] Reactions not only to actual contexts in life but also against the routine ways of reacting to them.

are usually made to get over it. Man here asserts not only his character as a self-conscious being, but also his other unique feature of being spiritual, his spirituality consisting in this capacity to rise above selfish motives. That is, art and morality involve a criticism of life as it is commonly led; but the criticism is not such as leads to the abandonment of life's activities. They only aim at purifying the desires and impulses underlying those activities by purging them of all taint of selfishness.

We shall now try to find out how far art and morality can succeed in their aim of securing complete unselfishness. To take up morality first. It is clear that a person does not earn the title to be described as unselfish, if he acts disinterestedly only occasionally. We do not call a man charitable if, once in a while, he gives a few coins to the poor. Charity must become a predominant, if not a constant, feature of his conduct towards the needy. Similarly, here also a man should be disinterested in whatever he does, if he is to be regarded as unselfish. Further, it must become a fixed habit with him so that he acts unselfishly without deliberation and almost instinctively. It must cease to be the result of conscious effort, and become instead the expression of a permanent attitude of mind. Let us see whether the stimulus to moral action is adequate to achieve this end. There is first of all the spiritual instinct in man but for which such activity would be altogether inexplicable. It would be impossible to make a non-moral being moral, whatever be the nature of the means adopted thereto. But this instinct does not, practically speaking, count for much. What counts more is the force of example. The example may be that of persons actually before us as in the case of our parents and teachers, or of those like Rāma and Buddha whose memory is preserved for us in religious tradition or history. These examples, indeed, go a long way and are sufficient to guide us ordinarily. But new situations arise in life, or there will be a conflict of duties, where they may fail us. Here arises the necessity for our exercising independent reflection which means that the need for unselfish behaviour is prominently brought before our mind. That is to say, however long one may practise unselfishness, one will not wholly transcend the necessity for fresh reflection. Such reflection may conceivably lead us astray; but even granting that it does not, it will mean conscious effort. Our own moral intuition must help us on such occasions; but that, from what we stated above regarding the spiritual instinct, may not. In other words, if the highest form of moral activity is that in which unselfishness appears as purely incidental to the purpose which that activity serves, that state is never attainable by common morality. It can never transcend the stage of conscious strife and become the outward expression of an inner attitude, and so long as it remains thus, it cannot be said that the attitude of disinterestedness is fully established. It may appear that we achieve such complete unselfishness in art, if not in morality, for it is recognised that aesthetic experience by its very nature is completely impersonal. The end which the moral agent seeks, it may therefore seem, is found accomplished in art. But this impersonal attitude is transient and it disappears sooner or later.[2] There is a lapse from it into routine life—a reversion to the common mode of life, with its varying degrees of selfishness according to the character of the individual concerned. Moreover, even during the experience, the impersonality achieved is in reference to a sphere which is not actual but ideal, so that it is in a sense artificial. It is achieved in an environment which is outside nature, as it were.

Art and morality, as commonly pursued, not only fail to achieve their aim; they may also lead to the very opposite of it. Thus, in its anxiety to be unselfish, morality may adopt the ideal of asceticism which at bottom is only a form of selfishness. The ascetic may not, indeed, think of any advantage to himself, in the common acceptation of that term, in pursuing it; but yet his attitude amounts to one of selfishness in that he leaves the world to itself and becomes preoccupied with himself alone. If it does so, it becomes not moral life but its negation. Self-mortification represents the right attitude to adopt towards oneself as little as self-indulgence does. The *Gītā*, for example, stigmatises self-sacrifice which ends in tormenting the body as the worst of its

[2] It is possible to say that art means self-forgetfulness and not self-realisation.

kind (xvii.19). Asceticism is indeed necessary for all morality; and the spirit of self-denial is the special characteristic of morality as taught in most of the Indian schools. But it is positive asceticism and not negative. We do not mean by this that negative asceticism is necessarily indifferent to others' suffering, for even those that follow it may be altruistic; but their altruism is external to their asceticism, while the positive variety of it makes it an essential part of it, the ascetic ideal there being reached in the very process of carrying out altruistic activity. Likewise, art too has a tendency, as it is commonly pursued, to degenerate into mere pleasure-seeking—emphasising, as the hedonist does, the element of joy in artistic experience to the neglect of that of impersonality. It then becomes reduced to epicureanism and so far unsocial. If morality becomes negative, art thus becomes self-centred. This is probably the reason why so much of art, in actual practice, is made to lean upon religion. But the nature of art is such that it is not at all necessary for it to do so in order to avoid such degeneration. To transform art into a mode of true spiritual experience through the subject-matter is to elevate it indirectly, while what is wanted is to derive such experience from it directly. It can serve that purpose by itself—by a direct idealisation of nature and life and in isolation from any religious faith. Just as by becoming purely ascetic, morality contradicts itself, art also by becoming self-centred contradicts itself, since the artistic attitude, like the moral, should be absolutely unselfish. Both the ascetic and the epicure leave the world to itself in their concern for themselves.

The reason for straying away from the correct path, despite the right instinct, is a lack of clarity in regard to the precise nature of unselfishness. Now unselfishness does not mean the complete repression of the self; it only means the conquest of the lower self by the higher. It is the failure to realise the distinction between them and its significance that accounts for the deflection of the moral aim towards asceticism. We cannot enter here into an explanation of the nature of these two selves. We shall only remark that unselfishness is as much positive as negative; and that, if asceticism is wrong it is because it overlooks the positive aspect of it and becomes purely negative. It is a similar lack of clarity about the true nature of the self that explains the vulgar view of art that it is a mere means to pleasure. The self does not stand isolated, but is through and through social. It is the failure to recognise this fact that makes the pursuit of art unsocial and self-centred. The urge to morality and to the contemplation of art is quite sound; and it points, as such, to a true end. But that end, being implicit, is only dimly felt and not clearly understood. Until it becomes clarified, there remains the danger of art and morality missing their true aim.

A knowledge of the distinction between the lower and the higher selves is not, however, sufficient by itself to ensure complete success either in art or morality. To take the latter first: It may do, so far as what are called self-regarding virtues are concerned. But morality means much more than these virtues. It signifies in the main a reaction to an objective situation, which is essentially social. Moral actions do not take place in the void. Since such situations are necessarily relative, proper reaction to them requires a knowledge of the whole of the social environment in which man finds himself. That is, success in morality depends as much upon a knowledge of the objective environment as a whole as upon a knowledge of the true self. If it is the lack of clarity in regard to the latter that results in distorted views like asceticism, it is the lack of clarity in respect of the former that explains why common morality can never reach the goal. It regards each moral situation more or less by itself—in any case, not in relation to the whole which informs it; and the result is but a piecemeal or tentative solution of the moral problem. It is, no doubt, true that what is right reaction to a given situation is a matter for intuitive perception and not reflection; but such intuitive perception is awakened and rendered vivid only by a knowledge of the whole reality. It presupposes an *understanding* of the whole of which it is a phase. We may, and do, often react rightly; but we are then in the region of mere instinct or *practical* insight which may fail us at any time and not in that of *rational* insight. Hence the need for complete knowledge. Similarly, in the case of art also. If it is the ignorance of the true character of the self that accounts for wrong indulgence in art, it is inability to direct commune with nature that requires an imaginative situation for losing oneself in its contemplation. In both cases then, a clarification of the ideal of unselfishness and a definite world-view are necessary. They are possible only through right knowledge of the whole of reality or, in any case, as in the Nyāya, of that part of it which bears on the self and its environment. Such knowledge defines the ideal towards which one ought to progress and also prevents deflection from it. Here we see the need for art and morality having a metaphysical foundation.

We shall now try to see how such knowledge, granting that it has been properly assimilated, affects the pursuit of art and morality. Moral action, as we have pointed out, is commonly determined by the requirements of particular contexts in life. If, at times, a wider view is taken, that is generally based on convention and is mechanical. Hence moral conduct ordinarily oscillates between conscious strife and unconscious convention. When the ultimate nature of reality is properly known the particular situations become illumined by it. Each situation, being seen in its proper perspective, acquires a new significance; and in reacting to it, the attempt is made to realise the whole through it. As a consequence, the reaction to it will be not only correct but also spontaneous. This secures joy in moral action in the place of strife, which commonly characterises it. That is, moral activity becomes not only unselfish but also spontaneously joyful as in the case of aesthetic experience. It is this influence of knowledge upon morality that Socrates meant when he said 'Virtue is knowledge'. The Upaniṣads also teach that that alone yields the best result which is done with enlightenment. Now as regards the latter. Aesthetic experience results from the contemplation of a fictitious situation. But it is a situation which is regarded as self-complete. With enlightenment, one sees the universe itself to be so, and can therefore derive the same experience directly from nature or some one or other of its numerous impressive aspects. Thus for the fictitious content of art comes to be substituted the actual world, transforming art into the mystical contemplation of nature. Whatever significance art has, the knower sees it in life and the world as a whole. Art becomes the passive expression of a permanent attitude, as morality is the active expression of the same. Further, the lapse from it to which we referred will, as a result of enlightenment, be into the right type of unselfish attitude, and not to routine life. The artistic attitude is then replaced by a moral one. That is, the same kind of attitude—joyful and impersonal—will continue after that experience as during it. In fact, it is no lapse at all. The only difference is that while the latter is a passsive state, the former will be an active one. The highest form of morality is that which is joyful and spontaneous; and the highest form of art is that which can transform nature itself into its theme. When these stages are reached, the distinction between them disappears except in one respect to which we have just referred. In these respects they differ finally but in none other. The attitude towards the world therefore remains the same whether it is contemplative or active.

It is this impersonal and joyful experience, which is constant, that is the ideal at which art and morality really aim. They both are synthesised in it. In the words of the poet, Beauty becomes Goodness and Goodness, Beauty. An ideal man, like Vālmīki, leads a life of which these are the two alternative phases. He is in contemplation; and in the intervals of contemplative trance he will be employed in philanthropic activity. But in both alike, he is spontaneously and joyously unselfish. Thus the aesthetic and the moral attitudes, as we commonly understand them, are more closely allied to each other than we imagine, and are only partial and provisional manifestations of the ultimate spiritual experience. Art and morality thus mean more than they are ordinarily conceived to be; and each, as it is commonly pursued, therefore achieves only half its purpose. But they indicate the essential character of the ultimate goal of human existence. In that goal, each attains a higher grade of excellence. Art and morality become metamorphosed in it and are also explained by it, though we deduce its nature through them.[3] The ideal of life for man is to remain in one of these two attitudes. But the two attitudes are

[3] The spiritually pure includes the morally good and the artistically beautiful.

essentially the same. It is impersonal, spontaneous joy in action and in contemplation; and that aspect will maintain its identity throughout the two phases. The Hindu scriptures, like the *Gītā*, sometimes dwell on the one and sometimes on the other of these two phases. The varying emphasis on them is explained as due to a difference in the conception of the ideal among thinkers—one attaching greater importance to one of them and the other to the other; but the best interpretation of it seems to be to take it as commending both as alternating phases of the same ideal.

8

The Number of Rasas

I GLADLY RESPOND TO the desire of Dr. Raghavan that I should contribute a Foreword to this book.[1] He has been carrying on researches in the field of Sanskrit literary criticism for several years past, and the material which he has brought together here shows how extensive is his acquaintance with the literature on the subject. He draws his data, it will be seen, from unpublished manuscripts as readily as he does from published works. The opinion formed on any aspect of the subject by one, who has devoted so much time to its study and whose knowledge of it is so wide, is of special value and deserves the careful attention of all scholars.

The particular problem considered here is that of the number of *rasas*, and its consideration necessarily involves the discussion of many important points relating to their nature and scope. As in the case of other problems investigated by the ancient Indians, we find here also an astounding variety of solutions. While some thinkers have held that there is but one *rasa*, others have maintained that the *rasas* are many, there being a wide divergence of opinion respecting their exact number. The usual view, however, is that there are eight *rasas* or nine, with the addition of what is termed *śānta*:

śṛṅgārahāsyakaruṇā raudravīrabhayānakāḥ ।
bībhatsādbhutaśāntāś ca rasāḥ pūrvair udāhṛtāḥ ॥

[1] *The Number of Rasas* by V. Raghavan, M.A., Ph.D., *The Adyar Library*, Madras, 1940.

Although Dr. Raghavan considers all these views more or less in detail, the main part of his discussion is concerned with the admissibility of *śānta* as the ninth *rasa*. His treatment of the question is quite comprehensive, and he examines it both from the historical and the aesthetic sides. A brief reference to each of them may not be out of place.

Owing to the uncertainty of our knowledge of the early phases of Indian classical literature, it is not possible to say when poets began to portray this *rasa*. The ascetic and mystic elements, however, which form its distinctive basis are very old features of Indian life; and they were highly valued by those who followed the teaching of the Veda as well as by those who did not. So we may assume that the *śānta* attitude found expression in literature quite early; and this is corroborated by the works of Aśvaghoṣa even if, on account of its chronological indefiniteness, we leave out of consideration the *Mahābhārata*, the usual example given of the *śānta rasa*. As regards writers on poetics, the earliest to recognise it definitely, so far as our knowledge at present goes, was Udbhaṭa. Possibly its recognition by them was even earlier. Bharata's view in the matter is somewhat doubtful, by reason of the unsatisfactory character of the *Nāṭyaśāstra* as it has come down to us. Some manuscripts of it mention only eight *rasas*, but others nine. The weight of evidence bearing on the point seems, on the whole, to be on the former side; and Dr. Raghavan adduces several convincing arguments to show that the references to this *rasa* in Bharata are all spurious. But it should be added that the *Nāṭyaśāstra* contains nearly all the essential points necessary for a theoretical formulation of it.

Before we pass on to the aesthetic aspect of the question, it is desirable to distinguish the emotive content or theme of a literary work from the aesthetic sentiment which, according to the prevalent Indian view, its idealised representation evokes in the reader or the spectator. Thus in the case of the *Śākuntala*, Duṣyanta's love for Śakuntalā forms the chief theme while the emotion, which it awakens in us as we witness the drama enacted, is *śṛṅgāra*. When we ask whether *śānta* can be a *rasa*, we mean whether situations in life involving the quietistic sentiment lend themselves to be similarly dealt with in literature. If they do, then *śānta* is a *rasa*; otherwise, it is not. The practice of great poets like Kālidāsa, which is after all the true touchstone in such matters, shows that *śānta* situations can certainly be thus delineated in literary works. In the last act of his play, just alluded to, Kālidāsa describes the tranquillity and holiness of Mārīca's hermitage in a manner which affects us most profoundly. But, however splendidly depicted, the *śānta rasa* occupies only a subordinate place there; and a doubt may therefore arise whether it can be the leading sentiment in a work, i.e. whether it can be portrayed in such a manner that it will impress us at the end as the predominant element in the unity of *rasas* which, according to the Indian view, every work of art is expected to achieve. Some of the works of Aśvaghoṣa, to whom I have already referred, show that it can be so represented. The *Mahābhārata* also, at any rate in its present form, illustrates the same truth, as set forth by Ānandavardhana in his masterly way in the last section of the *Dhvanyāloka*.

Yet there were theorists who denied that the *śānta* could be an art emotion. It is hardly necessary to examine their arguments when we have the practice of great poets and the opinion of great art critics to the contrary. But a reference should be made to one of them which appears, at first sight, to possess some force. This argument is that the attitude of mind for which *śānta* stands is altogether a rare one, and that its representation in art cannot therefore appeal to more than a very few. The objection, it is obvious, is based on the supposition that the test of true art is in the wideness of its appeal. The advocates of *śānta* brush this argument aside usually by saying that such questions are not to be decided by a plebiscite; but, by thus admitting the narrowness of its appeal, they seem to give up their position. Their conclusion that *śānta* is a *rasa* is irresistible. Indeed, it would have been a strange irony of circumstance if Indians, of all, had excluded it from the sphere of art. The way in which this particular objection is met, however, is not satisfactory. May it be that the contention that the appeal of *śānta* is only to a very few is wrong? No unwonted occasion in life—whether it be one of joy or one of sorrow—passes without bringing home to man the supreme desirability of spiritual peace. It means that the need for such peace is fundamental to the human heart; and this conclusion is confirmed by the pure satisfaction which the contemplation, for example, of the images of Buddha in meditative repose brings to so many. If so, the *śānta* mood is by no means uncommon; and the *śānta rasa* need not be an exception to the rule that the appeal of art is general. What is uncommon is the capacity in man to capture that mood and cultivate it, so that it may come to prevail over all other moods; but this deficiency does not matter so far as art is concerned for it has the power, of itself to enable him to attain, albeit only for a while, the peace of spirit which, as an old Indian critic has observed, even a *yogin* has to strain himself long to win.

Dr. Raghavan makes a valuable contribution to the study not merely of Sanskrit literary criticism but of Indian aesthetics as a whole, for the conception of *rasa*, though it is here dealt with chiefly in its relation to poetry, is general and furnishes the criterion by which the worth of all forms of fine art may be judged. I have no doubt that the book will be read and appreciated very widely.

9

The Problem of the Rasavadalaṁkāra[1]

THE RASAVADALAṀKĀRA IS one of a small group of *alaṁkāras*, generally recognised by the older writers on Sanskrit poetics. Some of these *alaṁkāras* are differently explained sometimes,[2] but they all relate to emotional states. It is with this, their common feature, that we shall be concerned here, and not with any of their internal differences. Our choice of the Rasavadalaṁkāra for specific consideration here is as a type representing the whole group, and what we say of it will apply *mutatis mutandis* to the other members of it also. We shall not accordingly refer to any of the latter, except when they illustrate some point that is of importance to our topic.

I

The significance of describing this as an *alaṁkāra*[3] is that it is an attribute of poetry—essential according to some, but only desirable according to others. As, however, poetry is defined as *śabdārthau sahitau*,[4] an *alaṁkāra* may embellish either its form

[1] I am grateful to Dr. V. Raghavan of Madras for his kindness in reading the draft of this paper and making suggestions which were of much use to me in revising it.

[2] Contrast, e.g. Daṇḍin's view of *ūrjasvi* (ii. 293–4) with that of Udbhaṭa (iv. 5).

[3] These old writers sometimes appear to grant the pre-eminent position of *rasa* in poetry, commonly recognised by later writers. Cf. Bhāmaha, i. 21, v. 3. But it is not a well-articulated view, and seems only to be a formal echo of what is found in Bharata (Cf. *Na hi rasād ṛte kaścid arthaḥ pravartate*) and is sometimes expressed by poets themselves.

[4] Bhāmaha, i. 16.

or its content. The Rasavadalaṁkāra, being an *arthālaṁkāra*, contributes to the beauty of poetry, not on its formal but on its content side. Our present purpose is to find out whether such a view is tenable.

We have stated that the Rasavadalaṁkāra embellishes the content side of poetry. Since this content is acknowledged here to be *vācya*,[5] the Alaṁkāra may be described as *vācyopaskāraka* or subserving the meaning directly expressed in poetry. But a question now arises as to whether this Alaṁkāra itself is *vācya* or not. Two views seem theoretically possible in this regard: It should be *vācya*, if we may judge, for instance, from Daṇḍin's definition of *preyolaṁkāra*[6] which is one of the group; and Udbhaṭa's statement that one of the means of communicating an emotion to the reader is to name it, for example, as *rati* or *śṛṅgāra*[7] lends support to the same conclusion. But, at the same time, the use of expressions like *sūcana* in this connection[8] by the latter, and *gamayati* and *gamaka* by his commentators suggests that the Alaṁkāra may not be *vācya*. Since, however, no *vyaṅgyārtha* is admitted by the older writers, it should, in that case, be indirectly known—through some form of inference, say, *arthāpatti*. As it is not easy to decide between these alternatives, *viz.*, whether the Rasavadalaṁkāra is *vācya* or not, we shall refer to both the possibilities in the consideration of our subject.

(1) Let us first select the view that the Rasavadalaṁkāra in *vācya* or directly expressed; and for this purpose, let us examine briefly the instance which Udbhaṭa gives of it:

iti bhavayatas tasya samastān pārvatīguṇān ।
saṁbhṛtān alpasaṁkalpaḥ kandarpaḥ prabalo'bhavat ॥
svidyatāpi sa gātreṇa babhāra pulakotkaram ।
kadambakalikākośakesaraprakaropamam ॥
kṣaṇam autsukyagarbhiṇyā cintāniścalayā kṣaṇam ।
kṣaṇaṁ pramodālasayā dṛśāsyāsyam abhūṣyata ॥

[5] We are overlooking the distinction between *vācya* and *lakṣya*, as it is not of importance to our purpose here.

[6] *Preyaḥ priyatarākhyānam* (ii. 275).

[7] *Sva-śabda-sthāyi-saṁcāri-vibhāvābhinayāspadam* (iv. 3).

[8] Cf. iv. 2.

These stanzas, which are Udbhaṭa's own, speak of Śiva's love for Pārvatī. They first state that, as Śiva pondered over all her surpassing beauty, love for her planted itself firmly in his heart; and then they refer to certain striking manifestations of it, such as a bristling of the hairs on the body, perspiration and the like. Here it is obvious that Udbhaṭa describes not the emotion of love but only its causes, consequences and accessories; and since, by hypothesis, the Rasavadalaṁkāra is *vācya*, it is these that we must take as standing for the emotion in his view. But they cannot do so, unless a materialistic view (which was repugnant to old Indian thinkers generally) is held of emotion, and it is identified with its objective accompaniments. So we must conclude that the emotion, in its essence, here remains uncommunicated.

(2) If, to avoid this difficulty, we suppose the Rasavadalaṁkāra to be not *vācya* but *arthāpatti-gamya*, that is, deduced in one way or another from the *vibhāvas* and the like, an idea of the emotion in question will certainly be conveyed; but it will be *conceptual*, and cannot therefore represent *rasa* which always means a *felt* emotion. For inference, as is well known, gives rise to conclusions of a generalised or abstract character, while poetry is expected to speak to us in concrete terms. The consequence is that the emotion portrayed comes to be known as only of a certain *type*, instead of as a fully particularised *instance* of it. In the hunting scene at the beginning of the *Śākuntala*, for example, Kālidāsa does not tell us merely that the deer fled in fear, but depicts the precise manner in which the fear manifested itself then and there. He makes it known to us, of course, that the animal was frightened, but he does so essentially through concrete forms.

Hence we may conclude that, in neither case, can *rasa* be classed under *alaṁkāra*. If the Rasavadalaṁkāra is held to be *vācya*, it will not yield the intended experience but only present its objective accompaniments; if, on the other hand, it is taken to be *arthāpatti-gamya*, the experience to which it leads will be very far from what is meant by *rasa*.

We may now draw an important corollary from the above. But, before we can do so, we should make a passing reference to a point which does not strictly fall within the scope of this paper. It is that some ālaṁkārikas, like Vāmana, regard *rasa* not as an *alaṁkāra*, but as a *guṇa*[9] of poetry. Since, however, *guṇas* too, like *alaṁkāras*, are conceived as attributive to poetry, that view also may be shown to be untenable on the reasoning adopted above. When we take this fact along with another, *viz.*, that *guṇas* and *alaṁkāras* are the only positive attributes of poetry, we may conclude that *rasa* should be an *alaṁkārya* (or *guṇin*) and not an *alaṁkāra*.[10] The only point to be granted for this conclusion to be necessary is that *rasa* is an element of poetic value—a point which is not disputed by any ālaṁkārikas, old or new. In other words, it stands for the 'soul' (*ātman*) or essence of poetry—not for what embellishes, but for what is embellished. That is, indeed, the view on the basis of which the later (*navīna*) school criticised the above conception of the Rasavadalaṁkāra; and, in taking their stand on it, they judged aright the place of *rasa* in poetry.

But misconceiving the status of *rasa* in poetry was not the only fault of the older (*prācīna*) school. They also failed to explain how *rasa* experience comes to be evoked at all. For, in trying to explain it, they landed themselves, as we have seen, in a dilemma, *viz.*, that either it remains unevoked in its essence or only an idea of the corresponding emotion is conveyed in purely conceptual terms. The later school has successfully avoided this dilemma by enunciating what is known as *vyañjanā-vyāpāra*, whose importance in elucidating the nature of poetry cannot be exaggerated. It means 'a process of suggestion', as it is commonly interpreted; but it also signifies more—that the reader should ideally reproduce in himself, with the aid of the suggestive elements and with that of his own feeling equipment, a mode of experience similar to the one, under the spell of which the poet has expressed himself in the form of the poem in question.[11]

[9] *Kāvyālaṁkāra-sūtra*, III. ii. 14.

[10] *Dhvanyāloka* (com.), p. 78: *Alaṁkārya-vyatiriktaś ca alaṁkāraḥ abhyupagantavyaḥ, loke tathā siddhatvāt.* This work will hereafter be referred to as *DA*.

[11] Cf. *Nāyakasya kaveḥ śrotuḥ samānonubhavaḥ*: *DA*., p. 29 (com.).

These suggestive elements are the *vibhāvas* and the like which he has portrayed; but, being only its outward accompaniments, they have to be imaginatively synthesised by the reader before they can give rise to the integral aesthetic experience (*akhaṇḍa-carvaṇa*) for which the term *rasa* stands.[12] According to this explanation, then, emotions are not *communicated* at all by the poet; he only suggests them and thereby helps their *waking to life* in the mind of a competent person, when they will necessarily be inwardly experienced by him. Here the later school has, unlike the earlier, rightly taken into account the important psychological fact that no emotions, other than one's own, can be directly experienced. But, when we speak of an emotion as 'waking up' in the mind of the reader, it should not be regarded as a revival of his *private* experience: that would, by no means, constitute *rasa*. For, though the process may eventually go back to impressions latent in his mind (*vāsanā*), the emotional experience itself, in virtue of the idealised character[13] of the *vibhvās* and the like or, to state the same otherwise, owing to the imaginative level at which the waking takes place, becomes impersonal (*sādhāraṇī-kṛta*)[14] and quite unique (*alaukika*).[15] This is the solution by the later school of the riddle of *rasa* experience.

II

The logical consequence of such view is to exclude the Rasavadalaṁkāra from the sphere of poetics altogether, for it is a self-discrepant conception representing an *alaṁkārya* as an *alaṁkāra*. And that is what the later school has; in effect, done. But Indian thinkers do not ordinarily discard an old concept, even when they come to see that it is not strictly legitimate, if they can profitably utilise it in any other way. Now an *alaṁkāra*,

[12] *Na hi vibhāvānubhāva-vyabhicāriṇa eva rasāḥ*: *DA*., p. 183.

[13] The very words *vibhāva, anubhāva* etc., imply idealisation; and they are not mere *kāraṇa, kārya*, etc., as the older writers persist in describing them. See, e.g. com. on Udbhaṭa's work, iv. 2, and cf. *Kāvya-prakāśa*, iv. 27–8.

[14] *Deśa-kāla-pramātṛ-bhedāniyantrito rasaḥ: Abhinava-bhāratī*, I, p. 292.

[15] Cf. *DA*., pp. 56–7 (com.).

by its very nature, forms a subsidiary category. It is what contributes to, or enhances, the beauty of something else. And it so happens that, even though *rasa* is intrinsically primal in character, it is sometimes found to subserve other suggested poetic elements—another *rasādi* or *vastumātra* (more correctly, only *rasādi*);[16] and then it may be *secondarily* described as an *alaṁkāra*. It is thus, not in its original sense that the name 'Rasavadalaṁkāra' survives in the later view, but only in an *upacarita* or figurative sense:

pradhāne'nyatra vākyārthe yatrāṅgaṁ tu rasādayaḥ ।
kāvye tasminn alaṁkāro rasādir iti me matiḥ ॥[17]

This is well illustrated in the following stanza where *karuṇa-rasa* serves to enhance the glory of a conquering prince, which forms the chief point of the poem:

kiṁ hāsyena na me prayāsyasi punaḥ prāptaś cirād darśanaṁ
keyaṁ niṣkaruṇa pravāsarucitā kenāsi dūrīkṛtaḥ ।
svapnānteṣv iti te vadan priyatamavyāsaktakanṭhagrahgraho
buddhvā roditi riktabhāhuvalayas tāraṁ ripustrījanaḥ ॥[18]

It should be added that this fact that a *rasa* may subserve another suggested elements of poetry was not a new discovery by Ānandavardhana or by any other later thinker. For Udbhaṭa (if not some other early writers also) admits what he calls *udāttālaṁkāra*, one of whose two varieties is based upon a recognition of that very fact. The *rasa* element is present in it; and yet it is distinguished by him from the Rasavadalaṁkāra, because that element is not of first importance there. The following is his illustration of it:

tasyādikroḍapīnāṁsanigharṣe 'pi punaḥ punaḥ ।
niṣkampasya sthitavato himādrer bhavatī sutā ॥

The stanza speaks of the prowess of Viṣṇu as *ādi-varāha*, butting repeatedly against the Himavān, and the mountain successfully

[16] See *DA.*, pp. 71 and 74 (com.).
[17] *DA.*, ii. 5.
[18] *DA.*, p. 72.

resisting it. Here there is a clear portrayal of *vīra-rasa*. But it is not portrayed for its own sake; rather, it serves to indicate the sublime constancy and steadfastness of the mountain lord.[19] Hence it is an instance of the *udāttālaṁkāra*, and not of the Rasavadalaṁkāra. It will be seen that, in this respect, it is exactly similar to the illustrative example of the Rasavadalaṁkāra cited above from Ānandavardhana. In this distinction which Udbhaṭa makes between the Rasavadalaṁkāra and the *udāttālaṁkara*, we may say, lies implicit an important aspect of the theory of *rasa*, as propounded later, *viz.*, that where the *rasa* element is predominant, we have the variety of *kāvya* designated *dhvani*; and where it is subordinate, we have the Rasavadalaṁkāra.[20] But he had not the necessary aesthetic outlook for rightly interpreting it, and therefore spoke of them both as *alaṁkāras*.

[19] *Na hy atra mahātma-caritam aṅgitayā sthitam api tv aṅgatāṁ gatam:* (*Vivṛti*).

[20] See *DA*., ii. 4–5.

10

Rasa and Dhvani

THIS[1] IS A thesis for the Doctorate of Philosophy in the University of Madras; and it was, if we remember rightly, the first of its kind to be approved by that academic body. It deals with Sanskrit Poetics or *Alaṁkāraśāstra* as it is called—a subject in which the Indian mind has achieved particular excellence. Its literature is vast; and, though the works that have been already published are numerous, there are many still awaiting publication. The theories propounded in them are diverse—as many as eight of them being of distinctive importance according to our author. The most important of these theories is that contained in the *Dhvanyāloka* of Ānandavardhana, a work of the ninth century A.D. It is known as the theory of *dhvani* or 'suggestiveness' which is based upon the view that what we may call the poetic ultimate is essentially incommunicable and can at best be only suggested. The present thesis treats of its subject with special reference to this work. The *Dhvanyāloka* is not to be regarded as merely a treatise on empirical aesthetics as several others are; for it develops its views in close connection with philosophical theories, raising now and again questions like the logical status of verbal testimony and the psychological basis of *śānta-rasa*. Another feature in which it differs from the common run of *Alaṁkāra* works is that the theory which it enunciates,

[1] *Some Aspects of Literary Criticism in Sanskrit or the Theories of Rasa and Dhvani* by A. Sankaran, M.A., Ph.D., University of Madras, 1929.

though in the first instance intended to explain the method and aim of poetry, is equally applicable to all forms of fine art. This is indicated by Ānandavardhana's own references to other arts like music for purposes of illustration. It is also clear from the nature of *dhvani* itself; for the means of suggestion need not be confined to linguistic forms, but may extend beyond to the media employed in arts other than poetry. Features such as these show that the *Dhvanyāloka* is a difficult work to comprehend; and the difficulty is considerably increased by the imperfect character of the only edition of it published so far.[2] But our author brings to its study a mind adequately equipped both in literature and philosophy. He also possesses the care and patience necessary for the examination of manuscript material incidental to such inquiries. The result is an essay which contains many well-tested facts and inferences, all set forth in a lucid manner. It is not merely on the expository side that its excellence lies but also on the historical and critical sides. In all these respects the thesis, though comparatively brief, goes deeper than any modern work we know on the subject. Of the several questions of interest considered here, we may mention one in particular, *viz.*, the relation between the principles of *rasa* and *dhvani*. The point is discussed at considerable length and its elucidation is a valuable contribution to the study of the subject. The thesis which represents apparently the first effort of its author, gives promise of much valuable work by him in the field of Sanskrit Research.

[2] [Other editions, some of them of single chapters of the work, have since appeared in Benares, Calcutta and Madras.—Ed.]

11

The Philosophy of Aesthetic Pleasure

THIS VOLUME[1] CONTAINS the thesis presented by the author for the M.O.L. Degree of the University of Madras. Its theme is Indian Aesthetics—a subject in which, as in so many others investigated by them, the ancient Indians have advanced numerous theories. Many of these theories are briefly referred to here; but the volume is chiefly concerned with the elucidation of the most prominent among them, which is known as the theory of *rasa*. The book is divided into ten chapters. The first three of them deal with the subject in a general way, and point out the importance as well as the antiquity of the *rasa*-theory. It is mentioned already in the *Nāṭya-śāstra* of Bharata, the earliest work on Sanskrit literary criticism that has come down to us. The next four chapters treat of the chief interpretations of Bharata's view of *rasa* and show how the latest of them, which we owe to Ānandavardhana and Abhinavagupta of the ninth and tenth centuries respectively, is the best. This view superseded all the rest, and has virtually dominated Indian literary criticism ever since. The next two chapters are taken up with the discussion of the exact significance of this theory, the extent of its influence and the modifications, all more or less slight,

[1] *The Philosophy of Aesthetic Pleasure* by P. Pancapagesa Sastri, with a Foreword by Mahamahopadhyaya Prof. S. Kuppuswami Sastrigal, Annamalai University, 1940, pp. xxiv + 324.

which it underwent in later times. The last chapter deals with the number of *rasas*, and considers in particular the question whether the *śānta* can be predominant *rasa* in poetry and in the drama. The view maintained here, on the strength of the opinions of great critics and the practice of artists of the first rank lie Vyāsa and Aśvaghoṣa, is that it can well be so.

The literature relating to this subject in Sanskrit is vast, and the author shows a close acquaintance with it. His exposition of the main theme, 'the suggestion theory' of *rasa* as he terms it, is very good. But there are large portions of the book which dwell at unnecessary length on matters that are well known to students of Sanskrit criticism. We have also come across a few doubtful or misleading statements. In dealing with Bhaṭṭa Lollaṭa's view, for instance, it is stated (pp. 64ff) that the *anubhāvas* or expressions of the emotions help the spectator in inferring the mental attitude of the hero and the heroine. But the spectator's conclusions in this respect have nothing whatever to do with the 'generation of *rasa*' in the actors or the characters represented by them. The *anubhāvas* seem rather to serve as to the hero and the heroine themselves to discover each other's frame of mind. But speaking as a whole, the book brings together a good deal of information touching the theory of *rasas*, which now lies scattered in many books; and its publication will accordingly be welcomed by all students of Sanskrit literature. The various indexes included in the volume, and the analytical table of contents will greatly facilitate the work of referring to it.

12

Some Concepts of Alaṁkāra Literature

THERE ARE NINE sections in this book,[1] and each section treats of some leading concept of Sanskrit Poetics. The concepts selected for consideration here, like so much else relating to this branch of Sanskrit study, go back to the *Nāṭya-śāstra* of Bharata, which is the foundation of most, if not all, of the Indian theories of poetry. Some of these concepts, like *lakṣaṇa* and *bhāvika*, are less familiar now than others; but all of them are more or less vague. Hence the need for explaining them. Their antiquity is part-cause of their vagueness, and the fact that they have frequently shifted their meaning in the course of history has contributed not a little to it. A satisfactory explanation of their present significance therefore makes it necessary to trace the course of these shiftings as fully as possible. The author brings to bear upon this aspect of the study his extensive knowledge of Alaṁkāra literature, including not only the portion of it which has found its way into print, but also that which is still in the manuscript stage. The discussions are throughout instructive, and they clarify many doubtful points in old Alaṁkāra works.[2] They also contain some interesting speculations as, for

[1] *Studies on Some Concepts of the Alaṁkāra-śāstra* by V. Raghavan, M.A., Ph.D. *The Adyar Library*, 1942, pp. xx + 312. (*The Adyar Library Series*, no. 33).

[2] e.g. *pallava* on p. 132, *rasa-prayoga* on p. 198 and *kriyākalpa* on pp. 264–7.

example, that concerning the origin of the earlier name of *jāti* for *svabhāvokti* or a realistic description of things (p. 94). In arriving at his conclusions, the author guides himself, rightly as many will think, by the view of Ānandavardhana and Abhinavagupta. They were great, both as poets and as critics; and in the theory of *rasa*, as finally formulated by them, Sanskrit literary criticism reached its high-water mark. We may refer to one small point in this connection. It is stated on p. 201 that the word *anitya*, in the sense of 'relative', came into use only after Ānandavardhana. But it seems to have that meaning already in *Jaiminisūtra* (I. ii. I), for it is explained there as equivalent to *aniyata* or *sāpekṣa*, i.e. 'not invariable' or 'dependent'.

Naturally details like these will have no attraction to students of Sanskrit in general; but their value to the specialist—whether he is studying advanced treatises on the subject or is engaged in research work in it—is great. The book is, indeed, a veritable storehouse of useful information for him. But it should not be concluded from this that it is of no interest at all to others, for the author in the course of his discussions now and then makes comments, appreciative or critical, on Sanskrit poets and poetry; and these comments, he always supports by apposite quotations. We may mention as an excellent instance of this 'practical criticism', as it is termed, the Section on the 'use and abuse of *Alaṁkāras*'. Occasionally, one also comes across bits of new and useful information as in the note on *Rāmābhyudaya*, a lost dramatic work of Yaśovarman, the royal patron of Bhavabhūti (p. 205). The book, as a whole, is a notable addition to the slowly increasing number of works in English on a relatively neglected branch of Sanskrit learning. The author alludes in the footnotes to one or two other works on allied topics as under preparation by him. We hope that they will be published soon.

13

Sanskrit Poetics

THIS IS THE first publication[1] of the Institute newly founded in Madras in the name of the late Prof. Kuppuswami Sastriar; and it greatly redounds to the credit of its authorities that they should have issued it so very promptly. There is more than one Institute of the kind in North India to direct and coordinate the work done in the field of oriental research. The lack of a similar institution in the South has long been felt; and now that it has been started, we trust that it will receive not only from scholars, engaged in oriental research, but also from the general public all the help and encouragement which it requires for fulfilling its important function.

The book under review treats of Sanskrit poetics. It was first published several years ago in the *Kāvyamālā* Series at Bombay with the classical commentary of Abhinavagupta, called *Locana*. Owing, however, to the meagerness of the manuscript material available then and its unsatisfactory character, the edition was far from correct. But the imperfect form in which the work appeared did not prevent scholars from discovering its great value, and Prof. Kuppuswami Sastriar was one of the first to do so. He had it included in the course of studies for the Honours Degree in Sanskrit of the Madras University, and taught it several times.

[1] *Dhvanyāloka* by Ānandavardhana, edited by the late MM. Prof. S. Kuppuswami Sastri, Sastra-ratnakara T. V. Ramchandra Dikshitar and Dr. T. R. Chintamani. *The Kuppuswami Sastri Research Institute*, Madras, 1944, pp. xx + 304.

In teaching it, he thoroughly corrected the printed edition with the help of old MSS. of the work which had by that time been secured for the Madras Oriental Library. It is in this corrected form that the original work and the commentary of Abhinava appear here. The present edition also includes a hitherto unpublished gloss on the latter, called *Kaumudī*, by one Uttuṅgodaya which affords real help in understanding this difficult work. To these, Prof. Sastriar has added his own annotations in Sanskrit, which he terms *Upalocana*. They are brief; but, as may be expected from his many-sided scholarship and rare critical insight, they are invariably illuminating. The usefulness of an edition, provided with such aids to study, is obvious and does not need to be stressed.

The work belongs to the ninth century A.D.; and its importance is well indicated by the fact that the view of poetry which it formulated has come to dominate Sanskrit literary criticism completely, superseding all the earlier views. It would be out of place, in a review like this, to enter into its details which are necessarily somewhat technical. We may, however, draw attention to two of its broad features. The first is the emphasis it places on what is known as the *rasa* theory. This theory not only points to the general importance of feeling in poetry, which is universally admitted; it also signifies that primary emotions (*bhāva*) like love, fear and wonder form its subject-matter *par excellence*, provided their treatment by the poet satisfies the well-known aesthetic requirements such as lifting them above the purely personal level. Other things than emotional states also have certainly a place in poetry. In fact, there is no object, according to the present view, which is not potentially aesthetic. But, speaking in the main, their purpose is to subserve the portrayal of emotion. The implication of such a theory is that poetry, when it is at its best, approximates to music. Both alike centre about emotion, and aim at inducing a predominantly emotional attitude in the hearer. The other feature concerns the method of poetry which, it is maintained, is not so much expression as suggestion or *dhvani*—a term which, it will be noticed, occurs in the title of the work. It is evidently deduced from the fact that emotions are quite indescribable, and that an idea of them can be conveyed only indirectly by depicting the more prominent among their outward signs. But when once thus deduced, the method came to be commended in the case of the other types of poetry also as a means of heightening their charm, although it may not be necessitated by the nature of their content.

The volume under notice contains only the first of the four chapters comprising the work. We are sure that the two scholars, associated with Prof. Sastriar in its publication, will not allow it to remain a fragment, but will secure whatever MS. notes he may have left behind and see that the rest of the work is published soon. We may also express the hope that the rest of the work is published soon. We may also express the hope that the Institute series will include the other unpublished works of the late Professor, such as his lectures on Indian epistemology delivered some years ago under the auspices of the University of Madras.

14

Process and Purpose in Art

MANY THEORIES OF the beautiful have been formulated in the past; and, though several of them may contain elements of truth, none is altogether satisfactory. This is the reason why the aesthetic problem still remains an object of fresh research and study. There has recently been published in America a notable book,[1] which deals with most of the fundamental questions relating to it. It shows the author's wide knowledge of the literature on the subject, and also his close acquaintance with masterpieces in more than one of the fine arts. His approach to the problem is not merely aesthetical; it is also philosophical. 'For some years now', he writes in the Preface, 'I have hoped to understand art and beauty not merely in a way which would be consonant with my own appreciations, but also in a way which seemed to me philosophically satisfactory.' But the book is written in a much-condensed style, and a single page of it will easily 'dilute' into half-a-dozen pages of an ordinary book on the subject. It consequently makes tough reading; but there is no question that a careful reader will derive from it much valuable insight into the nature of the aesthetic process—whether it be of creating beauty or of appreciating it. It is not possible in a brief review, like the present one, to do justice to its many merits. We shall therefore content ourselves with drawing attention to one important point in it, *viz.*, its view of aesthetic experience.

[1] *The Aesthetic Process* by Bertram Morris. *Evanston*, 1943. (*Northwestern University Studies in the Humanities*, No. 8.)

We shall indicate its main features best by contrasting it with what may be called the naive view of aesthetic experience. The latter starts with an analysis of the work of art into elements, which it takes to be distinctive of its beauty, and describes aesthetic experience as a form of delight resulting from their contemplation. That is, aesthetic experience is assumed here to ensue the process of contemplating beauty. According to the present view, on the other hand, process and result together form a single whole, and their separation is altogether unwarranted. The distinction between the two views is vital. In the one case, aesthetic experience is the end to which the apprehension of beauty is the means. There is, no doubt, a causal connection between them; but, otherwise, they stand apart as antecedent and consequent. In the other case, that experience is conceived as a continuous process of which means and end are but two phases. The only difference between them is that while in the first the creation or appreciation of beauty is in progress, in the second it is consummated. It is clear that, as thus conceived, means and end do not form a mere sequence as in the other view, but are integral. In fact, the means itself is wrought up finally into the end, according to the present view. It is this unified whole of experience that constitutes aesthetic value here and not mere delight. But delight is not excluded, for that experience, as aesthetic, necessarily involves a feeling of pleasure; only it becomes an aspect of the value here instead of being identified with it. That is, we seek art not merely for the pleasure it affords, but for the unique experience it brings.

The process of contemplation again is looked upon as active in this view, and not passive as in the other. That it is so is clear from the fact that the aesthetic attitude is critical. A competent spectator will instantly notice the least fault which may mar the excellence of a work of art. Those who regard the process as passive do so, because they start, as we stated earlier, with a ready-made object of beauty and naturally assume that its distinctive features, already there, have merely to be apprehended for attaining the aesthetic end. Really, however, it can be gained only through striving as much in the appreciation of art as in its creation. It implies that all great art involves a problematic situation, i.e. a situation whose meaning is problematic, and that its true significance will be revealed to none who does not insightfully follow the development of that situation until its latent tensions and conflicts are fully and satisfyingly resolved. It is to this consummatory stage that the author gives the name of 'beauty'. He frequently speaks of art as process, and product as beauty. He means thereby, if we have rightly understood him, that, like other values, the aesthetic also becomes a value only when it is realised in one's own experience.

Students of Sanskrit will recognise here a striking resemblance to a theory that has dominated art criticism in India for over a thousand years.[2] It is not necessary to enter into its technicalities to bring out the resemblance. It will suffice to refer to the significance of the title of '*rasa* theory' given to it. The word *rasa* primarily means 'taste' or 'savour' such as sweetness; and it has, by a metaphorical extension, been applied to aesthetic experience. The point of the metaphor is that both signify a process and that the process is, in neither, sundered from the result. If we neglect the almost infinitesimal time required to excite taste when a savoury thing is placed on the tongue, the process of tasting and the satisfaction that is its result are coincident. That is to say, experience is fulfilment in the one case as in the other. The metaphor has also a deeper implication. It points to the unity of aesthetic experience, however complex it may be, as also to its uniqueness for, when two or more tastes are properly blended, it is pointed out, the result is one single taste which surpasses all of them in its flavour. The appropriateness of selecting one of the 'lower' senses, rather than the 'higher', to typify aesthetic experience is in the importance of the element of feeling in art for, as psychologists tell us, that element is at a maximum in them.

But, as may be expected from the widely remote circumstances in which the two theories have been developed, the resemblance is only partial; and there are more or less important

[2] See Abhinavagupta's com. on Bharata's *Nāṭyaśāstra*, vol. I, pp. 286–91.

differences between them. To refer briefly to only one of them: the *rasa* theory not only points to the general importance of feeling in art, which is universally admitted; it also signifies that primary emotions (*bhāva*) like love, fear and wonder form its subject-matter *par excellence*, provided their treatment by the artist satisfies the well-known aesthetic requirements such as lifting them above the personal level. Other things also have certainly a place in art, and there is no object according to the Indian view which is not potentially aesthetic. But, speaking in the main, their purpose is to subserve the portrayal of emotions. In the best art of India, it is this emotional theme that is depicted. In Kālidāsa's *Śākuntala*, for example, it is love (*śṛṅgāra*); and the secret of appeal in so much of Indian music lies in the fact that it embodies the longing for God of passionately devout hearts. So far as we have been able to gather, the author of the work under review does not give the same paramount place to emotions as Indian aestheticians do.

15

Experience: First and Final

THE PURPOSE OF this book[1] is to determine the relation between two forms of experience—the aesthetic and the religious, which are apt to be regarded as hostile to each other. But, as the views commonly held about the nature of these experiences are widely divergent, it is necessary to state in what way they are to be understood here.

To take up aesthetic experience first. The author begins with a brief sketch of the history of aesthetic theories from the earliest times; but he sets nearly all of them aside as of little help to us in rightly understanding the character of this experience. Its secret, he thinks, was discovered only when it was investigated by the Italian philosopher, Benedetto Croce, in the beginning of the present century. There is no doubt that Croce's view of art is unique and shows several novel and striking features. This has been recognised by competent authorities ever since it was put forward. But our author goes much farther and (though, as we shall see, he finds it necessary to modify the view in some respects) claims that Croce has said there the last word on what is distinctive of aesthetic activity. However that may be, we should know his view, before we can follow the argument of this book. It cannot be made quite clear apart from his philosophy, but we shall try to state it with as little reference as possible to his general philosophical position.

[1] *Aesthetic Experience in Religion* by Geddes MacGregor, Macmillan & Co., London, 1947, p. 246.

Croce speaks of two forms of knowledge or the *theoretical* activity of the mind, which he respectively terms 'intuition' and 'logical knowledge'. The former produces images; and the latter, concepts or universals. Of these, logical knowledge invariably involves intuition and is dependent upon it; intuitive knowledge, on the other hand, is fundamental and independent. Similarly, he divides the *practical* activity of the mind or will into the economic and the ethical, which bear a relation to each other analogous to that between intuition and logical knowledge. Further, this practical activity, as a whole, presupposes the theoretical and is dependent upon it; but the reverse does not hold good. There are thus altogether four, and only four, grades of experience of which intuition, being the lowest, is the ground of all the rest; and the ethical, being the highest, is the most dependent of them.

It is intuition, in this sense, that Croce identifies with aesthetic experience. But what is its exact nature? Even an idle mood of ours in which we relax our mind and allow free play to our imagination is not, according to him, free from reflective elements such as judgments and suppositions, comparisons and contrasts. To get to the true intuitive stage, we have to go mentally a step lower, abstracting all such elements from it. It is this first mode of consciousness, when the image-forming activity of the mind goes on without any admixture of reflection, that is intuition. It is said to present things in their immediacy and to give us a knowledge of them in their concreteness and individuality, as distinguished from their general features; but it is a knowledge which, being detached from all logical considerations, is necessarily indifferent to the question of truth and falsity. Examples of intuition are 'this river', 'this raindrop', as contrasted with the concept of 'water'. Only we should remember that the particulars meant here are simpler and more fundamental than the corresponding percepts because they do not, like the latter, involve the distinction of real and unreal. From what has been stated, it will appear that this basic form of experience cannot be for us more than a moment's glimmer; but Croce holds that true artists and, with their aid, those who appreciate their works have the power to capture that momentary experience and, keeping it pure from reflective intrusions, persist in it longer than others can.

Now as regards religious experience: Its varieties, according to Dr. MacGregor, are almost inexhaustible; and he dismisses, as altogether unconvincing, views like that of the late Dr. Otto which maintain that all religions, without exception, contain a unique element and are, so far, one. It being impossible to discuss the problem of the present book with reference to this infinite variety of religious views, some specific form of it has to be chosen for the purpose; and the choice of Dr. MacGregor falls on Catholic mysticism. Its essential features are expounded here in the course of a learned and very interesting survey of mediaeval literature, going back to the Augustinian tradition; but we can refer only to a few of them in this review. Before doing so, however, we may draw attention to one of the changes which Dr. MacGregor, as already indicated, makes in the Crocean view. Religion, according to Croce, does not stand for a separate form of experience. It is for him a 'hybrid activity of the mind, in part art and in part philosophy'. Here it is reckoned as distinct, and also as the highest kind of activity in the development of man's spiritual life.

Some forms of theism take mystical experience to mean the attainment of absolute unity with God. But here the unity is such as preserves the distinction between God and the aspirant. It is described as an 'I–thou' relation. That is, the individual does not lose himself in God then, but only finds the fulfilments of his life's purpose there. This experience is non-sensory and immediate. It is also radically incommunicable. It cannot obviously be reached without a long course of training. Broadly speaking, the training consists in acquiring a knowledge of God and in loving contemplation of him. To confine our attention to the former: It is twofold—one, knowing, in faith, the truth about God; and the other, of rational reflection upon it. Both these forms of knowledge, owing to the ineffable nature of God, necessarily involve analogies drawn from ordinary life, such as thinking of Him, say, as our 'father'. It is this knowledge that should eventually grow into mystic experience; but it cannot have any place in that experience which, by hypothesis, is immediate, until the analogical images it involves, which externalise God, are rejected. Before explaining what this rejection means, it is necessary to refer to two other changes which Dr. MacGregor makes in the Crocean view.

First, Croce, as we have seen, holds intuition to be the ground of all the higher grades of experience. Only, being mingled in each with its characteristic determinations, it has to be isolated from them before we can get at it. But he does not accept in it any differences corresponding to those grades. All intuition for him is alike perfect. But here such a gradation is postulated, with the result that intuition comes to be viewed not only as basic to all other forms of experience but also as growing richer and fuller as those forms rise higher in the scale. Secondly, Croce denies that we apprehend any *external* reality at any level of experience since, according to him, mind is the sole reality and there is nothing transcendent to it. But our author argues at great length to show (without committing himself to any specific epistemological theory) that such a reality must be accepted in the case of every mode of experience. The significance of these changes to the present question is that our ideas of God are not without their own objective reference and that we can therefore also have an intuitive knowledge of Him which, as these ideas advance and become enriched, reveals to us His nature more and more clearly.

With this significance in our mind, we shall be able to see what the place of aesthetic experience is in religion. We have spoken of the need for rejecting the imagery of the earlier stages in knowing God, before mystic experience can be attained. After an examination of the statements of typical mystics in this respect, Dr. MacGregor concludes that the rejection is at first only of the analogical 'pictures', and that the corresponding aesthetic intuitions especially those that are based upon theological propositions and are therefore particularly relevant to divine nature, continue till the aspirant actually enters upon mystical union. They too are renounced then, but only temporarily as indicated by the fact that, when a mystic elects to describe his experience, he reverts to that very imagery. This shows that aesthetic experience is essential to the mystic state, viewed as a whole and distinguished from the act of mystic union. But, we should add, it is not sufficient, because there is also need, as already pointed out, for the activity of love. If mystic experience is incommunicable, it is so only in so far as it depends upon that element in the discipline, and not upon aesthetic experience.

The reader of this book cannot help feeling that the solution it offers is incomplete for, though the problem raised is general, it is discussed only in reference to what, after all, is a particular view of aesthetic experience and is a particular type of religion. But there is no question that the book makes a substantial contribution towards a general and final solution of it. The treatment of the subject is clear and methodical. The discussions are throughout on a high level; and the exposition is full of suggestions, which students of art as well as those of religion will greatly value.

The relation between art experience and religion is considered by Indian thinkers also, an we may close this review by making a brief reference to their conclusion. To those who are familiar with Indian thought, it is clear from the account given above of the approach to mystic experience, that there is a striking resemblance between it and the three ascending steps of spiritual discipline prescribed in Indian works—*śravaṇa, manana* and *dhyāna*, which respectively stand for knowledge of God, by faith, reflection upon it and meditation with a view to transform it into direct experience. Since *rasa* or aesthetic experience also, like this final one of *jīvanmukti*, is characterised by complete detachment and is accompanied by a unique form of delight, the two are described as similar. But there is one vital difference between them. It is the lack in the former of the knowledge of ultimate reality, which is essential to the latter (a deficiency which is made good here by assuming grades of aesthetic intuition that progressively reveal reality). To this, they trace the lapse from art experience which takes place sooner or later when, to speak generally, all the tensions of ordinary life return. There is a reversion to common life from the experience of *jīvanmukti* also; but it can, by no means, be regarded as a 'lapse', since the philosophic conviction endures then, with all its expected influence upon life's conduct. In other words, there is according to the Indian view, no direct connection between aesthetic and absolute experience, as seems to be supposed here. The discipline of the fine arts, particularly of music, is not, however, excluded from religion; but it is explained as only a useful aid to success in meditation upon the Highest (cf. *Yājñavalkyasmṛti*, iii.115).

Hiriyanna: An Appreciation

D.V. GUNDAPPA

This essay on Professor M. Hiriyanna's life and work was written by the late D.V. Gundappa, well-known scholar and writer of Bangalore. It has been translated from Kannada by H.Y. Sharada Prasad, a trustee of the Indira Gandhi National Centre for the Arts with the permission of Kavyalaya Publishers, Mysore, and the author's heirs. A few sentences from the obituary note that D.V. Gundappa wrote on Professor Hiriyanna in *The Hindu* have also been incorporated in the essay.

I had known of Professor Hiriyanna's eminence long before I had the good fortune of making his personal acquaintance. Among my preceptors was a humble schoolmaster under whom I studied Sanskrit grammar; he had been a student of Hiriyanna in the Teachers' College and he always spoke in awe about Hiriyanna's massive and meticulous scholarship. It made me look forward to the privilege of making his acquaintance, and the opportunity arrived around 1913–14.

A lecture by him had been arranged at the Shankara Math in Bangalore. The audience was not very large, fewer than a hundred, but included very distinguished persons. The subject was 'The Training of a Vedantin'. The manner in which Professor Hiriyanna expounded the subject elicited the unanimous praise of those present. After the lecture I approached him and sought his permission to publish the lecture in a biweekly English journal, *The Karnataka*, which I was publishing at that time. He was kind enough to agree to it and handed over his text to me. From then on I began visiting him.

Before becoming Principal of the Teachers' College, Hiriyanna, I believe, had worked in a high school and taught subjects like mathematics and geography. He wrote on these and other subjects in Kannada for the benefit of teachers undergoing training. These writings were first published as articles in a journal (Bapu Subba Rao's *Karnataka Granthamala*) and were then issued as books. One of them was on memory and another was on teaching methods.

Hiriyanna left the Teachers' College to join the Department of Sanskrit in the Maharaja's College of Mysore. Appointing him as Head of the Department was one of the notable acts of H.V. Nanjundaiya, the first Vice-Chancellor of the newly constituted University of Mysore. A special effort was made to comb the country for some of the finest scholars in each subject and bring them to Mysore. Hiriyanna's colleagues in that great galaxy were S. Radhakrishnan, N.S. Subba Rao, C.R. Reddy, K.T. Shah, Radha Kumud Mookerjee and R. Syama Sastri.

Hiriyanna was a man of few words. He never pushed himself forward. It took greatness indeed to recognise his work.

Hiriyanna had trained himself in Sanskrit in the traditional method. His father Nanjundaiya lived in Shivarampet in Mysore. Nanjundaiya's three sons, M. Hiriyanna, M.N. Krishna Rao (who rose to be Dewan of Mysore) and N. Sitaramaiya, all sat at the feet of a famous savant, Periyaswami Thirumalacharya, and acquired grounding in Sanskrit grammar, etymology and prosody in the old, oral way of learning. It is only after passing through this schooling that they took to the study in English. Such was the natural vitality and resilience of Hiriyanna's mind that the engrafting of the new and imported upon the old and indigenous in knowledge and criticism presented no great difficulty to him. The strength and soundness of these foundations were always discernible in Hiriyanna's erudition and in the precision with which he explained words, usages and concepts. Although I did not have an opportunity to sit at his feet to learn, I might narrate some experiences which illustrate his characteristic approach to academic questions.

I had once gone to Mysore for a marriage in my brother's house. I had written to Hiriyanna about my plans. He came to my brother's house a day after the wedding ceremony. 'We had expected you yesterday', I said. To which he replied: 'I could have come. But I thought I might not have an opportunity to talk to you as you would be busy with the other guests. I guessed you might be freer today.' After a few other preliminaries, I asked him: 'In our marriage ceremonies there is a rite called *neelalohita puja*. What might it connote? In the final verse of the *Sakuntalam* there is a phrase which says *Kshapayatu neelalohita*. Would it in anyway be connected with the ritual we practise?'

The talk turned to other matters. When Professor Hiriyanna left, I walked with him to his house in Lakshmipuram. There he gave me two or three notebooks filled with notes he had made precisely on the expression *neelalohita*. It was a joy just to behold his exquisite handwriting. He had put together the interpretations that various commentators had given to the expression as well as the numerous texts in which it had been used.

'May I make bold to ask you what is the conclusion you have come to?' I asked him after glancing through the notebooks. 'I have put together what I have found. But I find it difficult for me to pinpoint its meaning', was all that he would vouchsafe.

I recited a verse from the *Rudrādhyāya*

'नमोऽस्तु नीलग्रीवाय . . .' (16–18)
'द्रापे अन्धसस्पते दरिद्र नीललोहित . . .' (16–47)

Hiriyanna: It has its origin probably in the Vedas.
Could we not collate with verses like—

'नीलग्रीवा: शितिकण्ठा: शर्वा: अध: क्षमाचरा:' (16–57)
'नीलग्रीवा: शितिकण्ठा: दिवँरुद्रा उपश्रिता:' (16–56)

Perhaps it means that the world is full of mysteries, of things that cannot be explained, things that arouse fear; *neela* indicating mystery and *lohita* indicating fear.'

Hiriyanna: What you say deserves to be thought about.

I am narrating the incident to indicate the fastidiousness with which Hiriyanna approached any text. He went into every word, and made extensive notes about wherever an expression had occurred. He spurned facile explanations, and never imposed his own authority on others. Such was the precision of his scholarship.

Three words rise to the mind when thinking of Professor Hiriyanna: his scrupulousness, his purity and his serenity. Purity and serenity are perhaps implicit in scrupulousness, still it would be useful to mention them separately.

Scrupulousness means weighing the truth without committing the error of overrating or ignoring any aspect. *Pramā* means the correct measure. To appraise and understand something for what it is and speak out what one found is *prāmāṇikatā*, scrupulousness. To arrive at the Reality, it would be necessary to make a special effort to cleanse the mind of past prejudice and predilection. Habitual suspicion, anger and vanity are all impurities that obscure the truth. It is only when the mind is purged of them that it can behold the Real. Thus purity is a precondition of integrity.

So, too, serenity. Serenity means that the mind is not prisoner to any passion. When emotion of any kind, whether affection or antipathy, takes possession of the mind, it becomes incapable of seeing Reality without distortion. It is only when the mind is tranquil that the Real appears to us like a steady, unwavering flame. That is why the seeker of Truth must be dispassionate and pure of heart and eye.

Hiriyanna was a personification of the three qualities I have listed. He had no concern other than the truth. He never sought to please his superiors. In fact there were occasions when he spoke out the truth that was unwelcome to them and he had to suffer inconveniences as a result.

In speaking the truth, however, he was not harsh. Never once did he raise his voice. His tone was so modulated as to reach only those for whom his words were intended. As I said earlier, he was a man of few words. There was an abiding gentleness about his speech and manner—

> 'यस्मान्नोद्विजते लोकः
> लोकान्नोद्विजते च यः'

This seems to have been Hiriyanna's rule of conduct.

A few more words about his expository style. He observed the golden rule of economy. He believed that there was no need to develop an argument beyond a point and that a comment should be kept to the minimum necessary. He seems to have followed the guiding principle that Kolachala Mallinatha had prescribed for himself—

'नामूलं लिख्यते किञ्चित्;
नानपेक्षितमुच्यते'

—not to write anything that is not in the original; not to say anything that is unnecessary (that is, that the reader can surmise for himself).

Hiriyanna's two famous books, *Outlines of Indian Philosophy* and *Essentials of Indian Philosophy*, are both examples of the art of writing at its best. Each topic is dealt with at the right length. The sentences are simple and precise. The profundity of the subject and the lucidity and adequacy of the treatment combine to produce a mellow illumination in the mind of the reader.

Apart from the two classics, Hiriyanna has also edited some difficult philosophical texts and elucidated them for readers through his introductions and notes. Prominent among them are *Vedanta Sāra, Naishkarmya Siddhi* and *Ishṭa Siddhi. Ishṭa Siddhi* is a treatise on the acquisition of knowledge. It is considered an abstruse book and involves arduous exercise of logic. It seeks to answer the question how a thing makes its existence known. The technical word for it is *Khyāti*. Hiriyanna's introduction in English is a book in its own right.

He has also rendered into English *Īśa* and *Kena* Upanishads and large parts of the *Brihadāraṇyaka* along with Śankara's commentary.

Hiriyanna was as conversant with English literature as he was with Sanskrit literature. If he had not headed the Sanskrit Department he could well have been Professor of English. Shakespeare and Wordsworth were among his special enthusiasms. He subscribed personally to the London *Times Literary Supplement* and kept on file reviews which involved finer points of criticism. It was his habit to study the reviews of every weighty book that appeared.

It is beyond my capacity to pronounce on the depth of Hiriyanna's erudition. What even a layman could notice about him was his thoroughness. As I said earlier, even his handwriting, whether in English or in Devanagari or in Kannada, was itself a work of art. The letters were small but they followed the genius of each script and it was an aesthetic experience to read what he had written. The way he corrected proofs was a model for other authors. The changes he noted were tidy and the printer had no problem. He was equally neat and concise in his correspondence. There were no flourishes. If he replied to queries, there was not an extra word in what he said. The most recondite thoughts were expressed in elegant words and short sentences. It was an unadorned style, clear, classic and manly.

He had a library of well-chosen books. It was his habit to re-examine his collection every year and cull out books of secondary importance and give them away to those who might have use for them.

The room he used as study had the same Spartan simplicity. He spent most of his time in the front room of his house. It had a mat of fine weave on the floor and a low sloping desk, a bench, a stool and an easy chair. He did his reading and writing seated on the mat with the desk in front of him. Behind him there was a cupboard with five or six compartments. He kept his writing things and his files, all neatly arranged, in this cupboard. He offered his easy chair to his visitor and himself sat on the stool. If there were two or more visitors they sat on the bench. His library was to the back of this working-room. That, too, was a picture of neatness and order, with not a speck of dust. He cleaned the library personally.

He was also well known for his punctuality. Suppose I had an appointment with him at eight thirty on a morning. Exactly at that hour he waited at the gate of his house, with a pencil and note-pad in his hand. As soon as I arrived, he would conduct me to his study and wait for me to sit down before he did so. I preferred squatting on that mat. He would also settle down in front of me. The conversation would start with the matter I had come to discuss: 'You might perhaps like to look at the usage to be found in the sixth line of such and such a page in this book. . . .'

Only after the business had been completed would he turn to personal inquiries. There was no tittle-tattle and desultory chatter. The level of his voice was low and soft. Just enough to be heard clearly. There was no ostentation of any kind about him, no hint of his fame and authority. In his dress, in his speech and in his gestures he behaved as a man of refinement did when dealing with another man of culture.

Hiriyanna believed that in matters of philosophy, lived experience counted far more than book knowledge. He once told me: 'I have heard it said that I have not done justice in my "*Outline to some aspects of Dvaitism*" because of prejudice towards that school. The fact is that I lack personal experience of that philosophy. I have long wanted to find someone from whom I can obtain that experience. If you know of any Dvaita scholars who can provide me that insight I shall be glad to make their acquaintance.'

I mentioned the names of a couple of persons who had taught Sāmkhya and Tarka and who were highly regarded in Mādhva circles.

Hiriyanna: 'Do they teach from books or from experienced illumination?'

I was at a loss for an answer.

He continued: 'I have tried to study what could be had from the books. What I am looking for are persons who have lived Dvaita and have experienced it in their souls.'

A few months later I learnt from a friend that Professor Hiriyanna had located a very elderly Mādhva scholar and that he frequented his house.*

*I have been asked why Hiriyanna, who could write on sāmkhya and Vaiśeshika, could not also have written on Dvaita without insisting on personal experience. I would say by way of an answer that sāmkhya and Vaiśeshika are principally concerned with the nature of the physical world, whereas the Vedantas deal with the soul and demand personal experience. All the three major schools of Vedanta (Advaita, Dvaita and Viśiṣṭādvaita)

Hiriyanna had great regard for scholars of the old style. He had not a whit of the condescension that many modern scholars have towards the traditional ones on the ground that they chew the same old cud without intellectual awareness or breadth of outlook. He gave a ready welcome to traditional scholars and engaged in exchange of views with them. Two eminent scholars who were close to him were Palghat Narayana Sastry and Lakshṃipuram Srinivasacharya. His reverence was extended to the ancient religious centres at Śringeri and Kāladi. He often went there to attend the *Vidvadgoshthis* that took place there and awarded prizes to the scholars who passed the examinations held by them. Another scholar who was his compeer was Professor P.N. Srinivasachar who was for some years Principal of the Pachaiyappa's College in Madras and had written books on Viśishṭādvaita. I met him at Hiriyanna's suggestion.

If I said Hiriyanna was a generous man, some might express surprise. He gave in silence, taking care not to let his gifts be known. Many are the students who owe their education to his quiet and unadvertised generosity. He also assisted many philosophical and literary ventures. I know of an M.A. student of Sanskrit who received a monthly stipend from him. Let us call him A. Another student who was in need confided in A. A told him about the help he was receiving from Hiriyanna and advised him to approach him. The second student did so and Hiriyanna gave him an assurance of help.

There were three more months for A to complete his course. When he next went to Hiriyanna a surprise awaited him in the form of three months' money in a packet instead of one month's. When A showed his bafflement, Hiriyanna said to him, 'You had given me your word that you would not speak about the arrangement between us to anyone else. You broke it. I don't hold it against you. I am fulfilling my part of the bargain.'

Hiriyanna was a traditionalist in his conduct. He wore sacred ash on his forehead. He performed *pūja*. But he did not proclaim

---

are devotion-based. Their quest is God-realisation in the soul. Hence the essentiality of personal practice and experience when expounding Vedanta.

his religiosity. If he wore *vibhūti* it was for himself and not to impress others. His virtues were an expression of his inner evolution. There was no artificiality and effort about them. An old maxim he was fond of quoting brings out his character. Goodness, says that maxim, is like breathing in and out, it must be a natural part of life, and should not involve any conscious effort.

Hiriyanna lost his wife in his middle years. He spent the remaining years like a *tapasvi*, amidst the cares and toils of the world and in partnership with it and yet without attachment to it. The well-known teacher and pioneer of the Kannada renaissance, B.M. Srikantia, who was also a widower, often told me: 'Hiriyanna has shown me how to bear it. He has been a source of strength to me.'

He brought up a large family: daughter, son-in-law, grandchildren, brothers and nephews. He treated them with steady affection, helping them to tide over their crises with his sage counsel but standing above the battle.

I recall some correspondence I had with Professor Hiriyanna on some aspects of Plato. People who know me also know how impetuous I can get. God has not granted me even a thousandth of Hiriyanna's learning. I have mislaid the letters he wrote to me. In one of them he had noted the places in the *Dialogues* where he had found similarities with Vedanta. I suggested to him that these could be put together in the form of a book for the enlightenment of a large number of students. He was good enough to say we could work together on the project. The intention was a worthy one, but it did not have the Almighty's blessings. In my numerous commitments I did not pursue the idea.

Once I had used a particular expression, amending a more familiar one. Hiriyanna wrote to me: 'The word you have employed could perhaps be grammatically justified. But it does not seem to have the support of idiom. Perhaps you could consider using the form that is in vogue.' To some interpretation of a poem I had put forward, his reaction was similar. 'Perhaps you could think it over again.' It was always so. He never imposed himself on anyone. He wanted people to come to their own judgement after taking into account the various aspects involved.

Speaking of Hiriyanna's integrity one might say that he wrote without expectation of any kind of reward. There is a school of thought among our old literary critics that a poet composes his work from some aim in mind:

'काव्यं यशसेऽर्थकृते व्यवहारविदे शिवेतरक्षतये
सद्यः परनिर्वृतये कान्तासम्मिततया उपदेशयुजे।' (Kavyaprakasa 2)

—in expectation of fame of money. There might have been such poets after Kalidasa. It might have been the consequence of the belief that one of the duties of the king is to sustain poets and scholars. But we have numerous examples of poets who have written for no reward but only for self-fulfilment, for lightening the weight upon their souls. As an author Hiriyanna belonged to this class. He often quoted to me some line of Śureshwarāchārya. At the outset of *Naishkarmya Siddhi* Śureshwarāchārya says:

'न ख्यातिलाभपूजार्थं ग्रन्थोऽस्माभिरुदीर्यते।
स्वबोधपरिशुद्ध्यर्थं ब्रह्मविन्निकषाश्मसु॥' (1–6)

The key word in the verse is *svabodhaparishuddhyartham.* It means: 'Have I understood the work? Are there any short-comings or errors in my understanding? It is to find that out that I have set out to write.' It is when one sits down to write that one is able to assess the adequacy and accuracy of one's know-ledge. In order to write one acceptable sentence, you have to resolve a hundred doubts and dilemmas. This is *bodhaparishuddhi.* To write for the enlightenment and refinement of one's own self, that is *svabodhaparishuddhi.*

This was Hiriyanna's way. Within a couple of months of the publication of his *Outlines of Indian Philosophy*, I had the op-portunity of meeting a celebrated philosopher, a scholar who had laboured long on books on Vedanta and Western philosophy. In the course of our conversation I asked him whether he had been able to go through Hiriyanna's book. His reply was: 'I had occasion to see it in manuscript form before it was printed. His is authenticated writing. If I were to write a book in his manner, it would take me twelve or fifteen years.'

Hiriyanna wrote with great deliberation. He weighed every word, every sentence, before moving on to the next. Often he went back to re-examine what he had written and rewrote it. I have seen his corrections. He had no use for the 'never blotted a line' attitude. He had completed his *Indian Conception of Values* but was reluctant to hand it over for publication. 'It has to be looked at again', he used to say. For him what mattered was not volume but quality. He never uttered or wrote a word that had not reasoned thought behind it, he never interpreted a passage without the support of authoritative precedent or parallel. Likewise, he wanted that there should be no place for an inessential word. It was not necessary to expatiate on what the reader knew and accepted. To exclude the unsupported and the oft-repeated was part of his discipline. That is what gave such weight to whatever he wrote.

Besides *Outline* and *Essentials*, Kavyalaya of Mysore has brought out a few more of Professor Hiriyanna's books, mainly collections of his essays on philosophy and literary criticism. Some of the essays are in the form of extended book reviews and others are independent papers. They reveal the width and generosity of his outlook, his sympathy towards other writers, the graceful simplicity of his own style as well as the profundity of his scholarship.

His output was not vast but it was pure gold. He seems to have been gifted with the proverbial philosopher's stone which turned everything he touched into the yellow metal. The secret of his success, it seems to me, was that he husbanded his genius, did not spread it over too wide a field but concentrated it upon a few subjects which he made his own. One was *kāvya*, for which he had solid grounding in Sanskrit and English literatures. The second was philosophy, in which he mastered the six *darśanas* and all the theories connected with them. In particular he had a penetrating understanding of Advaita and Vishiṣtaadvaita. He had studied Western systems and texts that might help him in the evaluation of Vedanta. With all others, he avoided in his conversation and writing any tendency towards self-assertion. He had an exacting sense of what was pertinent. 'Na anapekshitam uchyate'.

He hesitated to venture beyond his two chosen fields, although there were several subjects in which he was interested. He was well versed in mathematics and acquainted with music. But he gave an impression of being uninvolved when they were discussed. There are many who seek to climb the throne of omniscience, the *sarvajña peetha*. They ought to take a lesson from Professor Hiriyanna.

Index